Managing
Change

Learning Made Simple

Lesley Partridge

AMSTERDAM • BOSTON • HEIDELBERG • LONDON • NEW YORK • OXFORD
PARIS • SAN DIEGO • SAN FRANCISCO • SINGAPORE • SYDNEY • TOKYO

Butterworth-Heinemann is an imprint of Elsevier

ELSEVIER

Butterworth-Heinemann is an imprint of Elsevier
Linacre House, Jordan Hill, Oxford OX2 8DP, UK
30 Corporate Drive, Suite 400, Burlington, MA 01803, USA

First edition 2007

Notice
No responsibility is assumed by the publisher for any injury and/or
damage to persons or property as a matter of products liability,
negligence or otherwise, or from any use or operation of any methods,
products, instructions or ideas contained in the material herein.

British Library Cataloguing in Publication Data
A catalogue record for this book is available from the British Library.

Library of Congress Cataloguing in Publication Data
A catalogue record for this book is available
from the Library of Congress.

ISBN: 978 0 7506 8454 5

For information on all Made Simple publications
visit our website at http://books.elsevier.com

 Edited and typeset by P.K. McBride

Cartoons by John Leech

Icons designed by Sarah Ward © 1994

Printed and bound in MKT PRINT, Slovenia

Working together to grow
libraries in developing countries

www.elsevier.com | www.bookaid.org | www.sabre.org

ELSEVIER   BOOK AID International   Sabre Foundation

Contents

Preface

Change is difficult to deal with. But it is inevitable. This book gives you simple techniques to:

◆ Recognise the need for change

◆ Help people through change

◆ Get ready for change

◆ Plan and implement it.

It is designed primarily for team leaders and supervisors – the people who need to make change happen. But much of the book is useful for individuals who are facing change at work or in their personal lives.

Lesley Partridge
2007

At Wadsworth and Wadsworth's they knew all about change –
its those small coins left over after a minor purchase.

1 Change happens

Introduction

Are you sick of hearing about the need to change, to reform the way we do things? If so, you aren't alone. We all know of examples of change just for the sake of it, and of change exhaustion, where people experience so much change they become overwhelmed and ineffective. Nevertheless change is everywhere, in business, in public life, in the workplace, and in our personal life.

Change is part of daily life and particularly of working life.

Change is inevitable, except from a vending machine.

Robert C Gallagher

In this section we look at the forces that make change inevitable, both personally for ourselves and for organisations. This will help you to:

◆ See the forces that influence change in your personal and work life

◆ Identify and prepare for changes that you can foresee

◆ Respond quickly to the pressures for change that you face.

The pressures for change affect the type of change that happens. We explore different types of change and their impact so that you can recognise the nature of the change you experience and plan how best to deal with it.

In the last part of the chapter we look at how two characteristics of change make change management distinct from routine management. To make change happen you need to be both a manager and a leader.

Do I have to change?

The short answer is 'yes'. Here's why:

No man is an island

Everybody is affected by influences beyond individual control, and is forced to respond to them. You can't ignore the rest of the world.

Think of some of the external influences that affect your private life:

◆ Mobile phones have changed the way that we communicate and the way that people expect to be contacted.

◆ Increases in world energy costs affect your transport and heating bills.

◆ Environmental concerns change the way you sort and dispose of your household rubbish.

◆ Changes in taxation and interest rates affect your disposable income.

◆ Traffic congestion affects when and how you choose to travel.

◆ The Internet has given people a different way of shopping.

◆ Same-sex partners can now have a civil partnership, which changes their legal and social status.

Activity

Think of changes you have made in your life in the past few years as a result of external influences, and note them down.

To keep being a contender

To be a useful contributor in your working life and an active participant in your private and social life, you have to stay up-to-date, not just with technology but with new ideas, processes and social attitudes. That may mean learning new skills or changing the way you behave.

You have to be able to respond to the people you work with and live with. You can be sure that some of them will be embracing change, even if you don't want to. Most people don't want to stand still while everyone around them moves on.

Changes happening

- My youngest child has just left home and my daughter has recently married. I've just been carrying on as though nothing was going to change. I didn't really think ahead. Now my children are independent, and they don't seem to need me. I suddenly have some freedom and I don't know what to do with it. At least not yet...

- We learned to use text messaging so that we could keep in contact with our daughter when she went on a trip to Thailand.

- I moved from Poland to the UK to get a better job and improve my prospects. At the moment I am working as an IT expert for a small company in London.

- I went on a team leadership course so that I could improve my chances of being promoted.

Activity

Make a list of your friends, family and colleagues, and think about changes that they will be experiencing in the near future. How will those changes affect you?

Karen	Moving out of London to live with new partner and start a new job	She's moving further away from me. I expect I shan't see her so often, and that she'll be very busy - with less time for me. Also I suddenly don't have somewhere to stay in London!
Jack	starts full time school	I'll need to help Jack to settle in his new school. I may be able to increase my hours at work. I need to talk to Fiona (childminder) and investigate after-school care
George	Unhappy at work	Not sure what this may mean for him or for me. What changes can we make?

To make life more interesting

Many people make a change because they are bored or dissatisfied with their life. A job may be dull or feel like a dead end. A person may no longer like the place where they are living and want to move somewhere else. People make changes because they crave adventure and challenge.

There are a lot of things I want to do with my life. If not now, when?

Activity

Think of a change which would make your life more interesting. It could be a simple change like taking up motorbiking or running, or it could be a radical change like moving to Australia. Make a note of the change and say *why* you want to make it.

The human condition

If you're in a bad situation, don't worry it'll change. If you're in a good situation, don't worry it'll change.

John A. Simone, Sr.

We are all changing all the time, by the very fact that we are growing older. So even if you are content with your life as it is now, it is going to change. Children are born, grow up, leave home. Relationships alter. You may get married; you may get divorced. Close friends may move away and you may meet new people.

A big force for change is changes in health. The change may not be negative. People give up smoking; get over long-term problems, perhaps by finding a new treatment; and become fitter. But of course some illnesses or injuries force us to change the way we live.

'I was a heavy smoker – a sixty-a-day man. Then I broke my ankle. During the enforced idleness I had time to take stock of my life and especially my health. I decided I didn't want to die young. So I gave up smoking. I'm proud that I had the strength to do it. Frankly, breaking my ankle was one of the best things that ever happened to me.'

Do organisations have to change?

Again, the short answer is yes. Pressure on organisations to change comes from:

◆ The outside world

◆ Sources closer to home

◆ Inside the organisation itself.

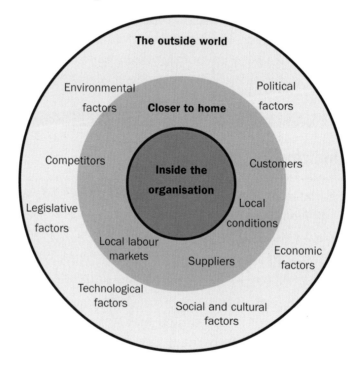

Organisations try to anticipate the forces in each of these areas so that they have time to prioritise and plan appropriate changes. This has to be preferred over waiting for the forces to have an impact and then having to react quickly.

The outside world

Every part of an organisation is open to external influences which can pressurise the organisation to change. We can categorise these influences as:

- **Political factors** – government policies and initiatives, attitudes to industry and competition, political alignments at home and abroad

- **Economic factors** – interest rates, currency exchange rates, consumer expenditure, inflation

- **Social and cultural factors** – where people live, education and health, social mobility, social and cultural attitudes to work, home and community life, and behaviour

- **Technological factors** – new products and services, access and availability of new technologies, existing technologies becoming outdated

- **Legislative factors** – employment law, taxation law, health and safety legislation

- **Environmental factors** – pollution control, water, transport and development policies, waste disposal

… or any combination of these.

These are known together as PESTLE factors – from the first letter of each word. Organisations use these factors to analyse the forces in the outside world that may lead to changes in the organisation.

Shell and Gazprom

In December 2006 the Russian state oil company, Gazprom, took control of Shell's Sakhalin 2 gas field project after a deal with Shell that gave it a 30 per cent stake. Part of the deal for Shell is Gazprom's help with the long-running campaign by local government ministries to fine Shell over its alleged environmental violations, with potential fines of up to $30 billion.

Analysts see the move as part of a wider campaign by the Russian government to bring oil and gas supplies back under state control.

As a consequence analysts have downgraded Shell's oil reserves and expressed doubts as to whether Shell can retain operational control of the project. The uncertainty has resulted in a lower share price putting further pressure on Shell.

This is a good example of factors combining to influence change in a large international business.

Paternity leave

At the time of writing, the UK government is proposing to give fathers up to six months' paternity leave if the mother returns to work. It is currently two weeks. This proposal is alarming small businesses, with the British Chamber of Commerce describing it as 'an administrative nightmare'. The fear is that small firms could lose key staff for months at a time and incur additional costs for administering the scheme, hiring temporary staff and lost productivity. The Federation of Small Businesses says that some will not be able to cope. The factors at work here are political, social and legal, and if the proposals come into force they will have far-reaching effects on small businesses.

Analyse PESTLE factors

To anticipate the kind of changes an organisation is likely to have to make in the future, you analyse PESTLE factors to look for developments that will affect it. Sources of information include newspapers and online news services which report and analyse national and global trends and events. Focus on a few factors that will have the greatest impact on a part of the organisation that interests you. For example if you are interested in fundraising for a charity, key factors could include economic (overall confidence among consumers), political (policies that affect funding to the charitable sector), legislative (fundraising rules and tax incentives for giving), and social and cultural (trends and attitudes towards giving; attitudes to the type of charity you are interested in).

Activity

Think of an organisation you know. Note down any external PESTLE factors that have caused it to change. Briefly describe the factor and what changed.

The factors you noted will depend on the nature of the organisation. However, here are some factors that influence many organisations:

◆ Anti-ageism employment guidelines

◆ Availability of low-cost labour from new EU member states

- Increased use of the Internet by consumers because of the wider availability of broadband Internet services
- Increases in identity theft and Internet fraud
- Cheap manufactured goods from China and developing countries
- Increases in fuel and energy costs
- Attitudes and laws concerning recycling and waste disposal.

Closer to home

Organisations of all sizes are also influenced by forces acting on their business or industry sector and in their local area. These include:

- **The pool of potential customers** – do they want the organisation's products and services? Can they get them cheaper or more easily elsewhere?
- **Competitors** – what action is the competition taking to steal the organisation's customers?
- **Suppliers** – does the organisation have a choice of suppliers and are they keen to get the organisation's business?
- **Labour market** – are there enough workers with the right skills?
- **Local conditions** – what's happening locally that affects the organisation's viability?

A small business

A high street shop offering specialist food items has suffered a downturn in sales. The owners identified the lack of in-town parking and its high cost as the main factor keeping customers away. As the local council's policy is to reduce traffic in the town and there are no plans to improve public transport, the owners feel forced to consider changing location.

Activity

Think of an organisation you know. How have the actions of customers, competitors or suppliers affected it? How have trends or changes in the local area affected the organisation?

Within the organisation itself

Forces within the organisation can also lead to change:

- A new boss might have a different style and approach or want to take the organisation in a new direction.
- A new strategy may be stimulated by an analysis of external forces and may involve:
  - ❖ providing new products and services
  - ❖ cutting costs
  - ❖ moving into new markets.
- Attempts to make the organisation more efficient by changing the way people work.

Changing work practices

The repair division of a large aero engine manufacturer services and repairs the engines. As a quick turnaround is essential for the aircraft operators, the manufacturer was unable to predict or budget for the overtime its engineers had to work. After detailed consultation with staff the organisation introduced a new performance system. Part of this involved a substantial increase in basic pay and doing away altogether with overtime payments. Engineers still put in the extra hours needed to get an engine back in operation, but now instead of overtime payments they gain time off instead. One engineer was able to take an extra three weeks' leave in the first year.

The change means that the organisation has to employ and develop more skilled engineers, but can now control its human resources costs. It has also involved a change of culture for the workforce, with a new emphasis on a work-life balance.

Change is inevitable both for us as individuals and for our organisations. However, change can happen in different ways. We look at this next.

Types of change

The pressures for change influence the type of change experienced – its speed and scope, and how it is introduced and planned. Change can be anywhere on a scale from radical to gradual. It may be imposed from above or initiated from below.

Types of change

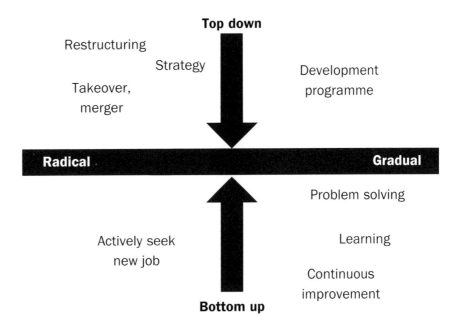

Given that change is everywhere, most people will have experience of types of change at each end of the radical-gradual scale. We'll look at these in more detail. We'll also look at particular kinds of radical and gradual change.

Radical change

Radical change is akin to revolution – usually rapid and with a broad scope. It happens quickly and has far-reaching effects through the whole or part of the organisation. It is characterised by a major shift in the way people work or act, perhaps requiring different values and attitudes. Such a change may arise out of a crisis or a determination to forestall a future crisis. When it becomes clear that the current path will not lead to the required destination it is often necessary to change direction completely.

11

Radical change is often marked by a decision to make a distinct break from a current situation in order to reach a desired future situation. The breakpoint decision can bring significant disruption and turmoil, but it creates new conditions and leads to a process of change in order to achieve the desired future situation.

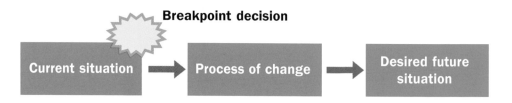

A personal example of a breakpoint decision could be accepting a new job in a different organisation. Organisational examples include a decision to outsource contact centre operations; a merger or takeover; a strategic decision to restructure the organisation or part of it; or approval to introduce new technology.

The diagram of radical change suggests that the process of change is finite, and that once the desired future situation is reached then the change process will end and the new situation will become established as normal practice. However, some radical change is open-ended.

Open-ended change

Open-ended change is characterised by a radical change, followed by soon after by another, and perhaps more to come.

In open-ended change, it is clear that the organisation has to adapt in order to meet the demands made on it. There may even be a clear picture of what the organisation should be in future. But no one knows precisely how to move it from its current situation to the desirable future situation. There is no sure recipe for success.

In this case changing the organisation means planning and implementing a change, monitoring what happens, reviewing progress, then trying another change, reviewing it and trying another.

Open-ended change may be experienced in large complex organisations such as the National Health Service.

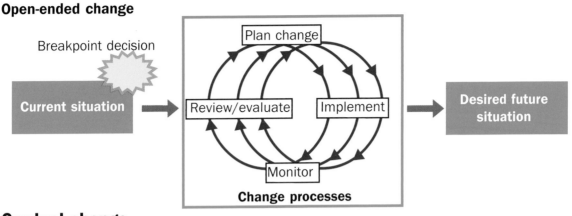

Open-ended change

Breakpoint decision

Current situation

Plan change

Review/evaluate   Implement

Monitor

Change processes

Desired future situation

Gradual change

Gradual change is evolutionary – making small adjustments to improve a product or service, to cut costs or improve efficiency, or to better suit someone's needs. Over the long term, gradual change can have a significant impact. Gradual change is often integrated into routine activities. It includes reviewing and addressing gaps between current practice and ideal practice, problem-solving and learning.

A personal example of gradual change is the way that the relationship between a parent and child develops as the child grows to maturity and adulthood.

Top-down and bottom-up change

Top-down change is imposed by others, usually those in power. In an organisation, for example, change may be initiated, planned and led by the senior management team. But the plans for change are carried out by all levels of the organisation and its effects are felt throughout. Top-down change is often radical when the leaders of an organisation feel it has to make a break with the past to achieve its aims. Top-down change does not have to be rapid. A development programme initiated by senior management can take time to implement, but it may have a profound long-term effect on performance and attitudes.

Bottom-up change is planned and led by the people who carry it out. These people understand their part of the organisation and know their customers needs, and so are best placed to find ways to make improvements. Bottom-up change is often gradual, involving small incremental changes.

Continuous improvement

Continuous improvement is an important form of gradual change, which is planned and carried out by small teams – rather than imposed from above. It is a systematic, endless process, shown by a cycle of Plan, Do, Check and Act.

◆ **Plan** – analyse a problem and find a solution

◆ **Do** – implement the solution

◆ **Check** – review the results against the desired results and carry out action to make corrections as appropriate

◆ **Act** – build the solution into standard practice, learning lessons from the experience.

Then the process starts again.

The theory

The PDCA cycle was first described by W. Deming, an early expert on the quality movement, and one of the first to explore continuous improvement.

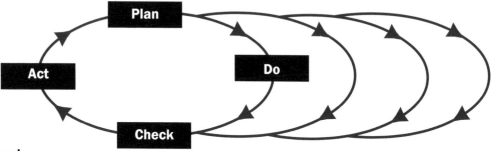

The PDCA cycle

The basis of continuous improvement is to:

◆ Examine current operations and practice against the needs and expectations of customers and the organisation's priorities

◆ Identify any gaps in performance

◆ Find ways of closing these gaps

◆ Make changes and review progress.

Continuous improvement schemes can be motivating, as they give people doing the work the opportunity to solve problems and make improvements in their own work area and then see those improvements in action.

It is important for everyone to recognise that the process is continuous. Customer needs and organisational priorities change over time, and may become more demanding. The expertise and technology available to meet those needs also develop, giving scope for further refinements.

Continuous improvement enables an organisation to improve the quality of its products and services, its processes and activities. The discipline of the process also gives the organisation some flexibility, so that it is able to anticipate and respond to future needs. However, continuous improvement does not replace the need for radical change. When the forces for change outside the organisation trigger a new strategic direction, there may be radical top-down change.

Activity

Note down a few examples of change you have experienced. You could draw on personal changes and changes at work. Then consider how you would categorise each change:

◆ Assess where each change lies on the radical-gradual scale by taking account of the speed and scope of the change.

◆ Note whether it was imposed on you – top-down change – or whether it was something you initiated or generated – bottom-up change.

◆ Note also whether each change was finite or whether it is ongoing. Can you describe it as continuous improvement? Or is it more like radical open-ended change?

It is useful to be able to distinguish between different types of change, because the type of change will have an impact on the levels of control and risk experienced and the skills and techniques used to manage it.

Making change happen

Two characteristics of change make change management distinct from routine management: control and risk.

Control and risk

Change always has some risk attached, because people never have full control over events.

Control is the power to bring about the change desired.

Risk is the likelihood that things will go wrong and the consequences of them doing so.

Activity

Think about the changes you have identified. For each one, consider these questions:

◆ How much control did you feel you had to bring about the desired outcome?

◆ How much risk did the change involve?

◆ Which type of change do you feel is more manageable?

◆ Which type of change do you feel is easier to deal with?

Radical top-down change carries a high level of risk because of the ambitious nature of the change. There are many uncertainties and variables and it is difficult to control events. Indeed, the level of control felt by the people involved is likely to be low:

◆ The people implementing the change feel they have lost control because the change is imposed on them. In addition, their ability to influence the change process is limited.

◆ Those initiating the change may also feel that they don't have enough control – after all, they depend on others to carry out the change and although they have power to direct some events, they are not all-knowing or all-powerful.

In contrast, gradual, bottom-up change allows a reasonably high level of control and a reasonably low level of risk. This is owing to the small scope and scale of the change and the fact that it is initiated and led by the people who also carry it out.

The level of risk and control experienced in change, particularly in radical change, mean that change can be difficult for people to deal with. We look at responses to change in the next chapter. But first consider how the characteristics of control and risk affect the way change is managed.

Managing change

> To manage change you must be both manager and leader.

In order to have some control over the process of change and so minimise the risks you need to manage the change. This means you need to:

◆ Decide where you want to go (your desired future situation)

◆ Understand where you are now (your current situation)

◆ Work out what you need to do to move from where you are now to where you want to be (the process of change)

◆ Keep track of progress and make course corrections so that you end up where you want to be (the process of change).

Managing involves:

◆ Planning

◆ Organising

◆ Coordinating

◆ Monitoring

◆ Reviewing.

The essence of management is to **plan** and **control** your resources effectively.

Managing small changes may be relatively straightforward. But managing radical change often means taking a step into the unknown. Even when the desired outcome is clearly stated and well-understood, it is often difficult to know what action is needed to achieve it.

The people who plan change rarely have complete and accurate information. They have to work with what is available. They may expect that a particular action will lead to a particular result, but there is always doubt. This is especially so when the change is complex and involves coordinating lots of different people, resources and activities and taking account of likely events and risks.

The need for leadership

The nature of change means dealing with ambiguities and anxieties that accompany the lack of control and heightened risks. Management skills are necessary. But the difficulty of planning and controlling change means that management skills are not enough. Managers must be also be leaders.

Where managers focus on the task, leaders focus on people:

Managers	Leaders
♦ Achieve results through other people	♦ Enable people to achieve results
♦ Give attention to the task that other people carry out	♦ Give attention to people so they can carry out the task
♦ Plan and control	♦ Inspire and enable

Leadership is needed because it is people who make change happen, who can achieve the desired future situation. It is people who can find creative ways to overcome the unpredictable obstacles and hitches that can stop change in its tracks.

But most people don't like change, especially when it is imposed on them. As you'll see in the next chapter, change is an uncomfortable process for many. People often resist change at first and need time to adapt to it.

So leadership plays a key role in helping people to work positively in support of the change.

Leadership involves:

◆ Influencing and persuading

◆ Supporting and encouraging

◆ Building motivation

◆ Facilitating and enabling

◆ Involving people

◆ Encouraging participation.

To lead change you need the ability to plan and control resources – a management focus. You must also be able to lead your team to work to achieve the desired future situation – a leadership focus.

Leading change

This book looks at how to combine a management and leadership focus to make change happen.

Summary

◆ People have to change because they cannot live in isolation, they want to remain contenders, and change makes life interesting.

◆ Organisations have to change because they are subject to pressures from the outside world, the sector, their local area, and from within.

◆ Change can be anywhere on a scale from radical to gradual.

◆ Change may be top-down or bottom-up.

◆ Continuous improvement is an example of gradual, bottom-up change.

◆ Change always involves risk, because you never have full control over events.

◆ To make change happen you need to be both manager and leader.

2 Responding to change

Introduction

It is usually up to people to carry out a change. They can make it work or they can work against it so that it does not bring about the hoped-for results. People have to be on the side of change if it is to have a chance of succeeding.

But change can stir difficult emotions and be stressful; and many people do not cope well with it. With some understanding of responses to change you can find ways to help people be ready to make change work.

In this chapter we look first at the kinds of emotions people experience when faced with change and the reasons why many find change so hard. We look at some of the things you can do to deal with your own concerns about change.

We then explore the stages people tend to go through to come to terms with change. It can be reassuring to find that these stages are usually dynamic.

We look at the leadership skills you can use to help people to move through these stages.

To be able to support your team effectively you need to take care of yourself. We look at how to have a positive attitude, avoiding stress and maintaining a work-life balance.

Responses to change

Think of recent changes you have experienced – preferably one change you made for yourself and one that was imposed on you. For each one make brief notes in answer to these questions:

◆ What was the change?

◆ How did you feel about the change at the beginning?

◆ How easy was it for you to change?

◆ How do you feel about the change now?

Everyone is different. See if any of these comments made by people facing change strike a chord with you.

'I feel like I've lost control of my life.'

'I like things just fine as they are.'

'One minute I'm excited, the next I'm anxious.'

'I'm worried about what it will mean for me.'

'What happens if it doesn't work out?'

'I can't cope with another upheaval!'

Many people feel anxious or stressed when dealing with change. Even when the change is welcome, such as a promotion or a new relationship, it can be difficult to adjust to the new situation.

Why do people find change so hard?

Here are some of the answers to this question. Change means:

◆ Uncertainty

◆ Giving up something

◆ Increased workload

◆ Learning.

Change means uncertainty

Change involves moving from a known situation to a new one, so uncertainty is one of the most obvious characteristics of change. Even with the most thorough preparation and planning, there is no guarantee that the change will bring the desired result.

The way people respond to change depends to some extent on where they sit on the certainty-uncertainty spectrum at that time.

Certainty	Uncertainty

At the certainty end of this spectrum you are settled and stable. You know where you are, what to do and how to do it. It is familiar. It feels safe and sure. You know what to expect almost as if you can predict what your future will look like.

Uncertainty is unfamiliar territory. There is little that can be taken for granded and few routines. You don't know what to expect, you can't predict what the future will look like and have to make your way into the unknown. Uncertainty can feel stimulating and exciting.

One person may prefer certainty – the reassurance of stability; another may prefer some uncertainty – the challenge of the unknown. Whatever someone's preferences, they are likely to feel uncomfortable if they are forced to move to another part of the spectrum.

Activity

Where do you prefer to sit on the certainty–uncertainty spectrum?

How do you feel when you are forced to move from your preferred position on the spectrum – either towards certainty or towards uncertainty?

People who enjoy the spice of uncertainty may feel bored and unsettled if their life becomes routine and stable. But those in this situation usually have scope to introduce uncertainty in their life, for example by taking up a sport, moving house, changing jobs.

People who are forced to move towards uncertainty from a preferred position of certainty may experience anxiety. By its nature, there is little opportunity to introduce stability into a situation of turmoil, and this can heighten the feeling that they have lost control over their life.

Many people lack confidence when faced with the uncertainty that accompanies change. They fear that they won't be able to cope, and they question their ability to succeed in a future which they can't envisage.

Those who are comfortable with uncertainty are likely to be more able to cope with change than those who dislike it. They may relish the challenge of change, and feel stimulated and invigorated. But even they may experience occasional doubts and anxiety.

Change means giving up something

All change involves some kind of loss. Even if you approve of a change and recognise that it will benefit you, there are often aspects of a current situation that you regret having to give up. For a start, there is the familiarity of a known location, colleagues or work practices. There may be aspects of a job or environment that were particularly satisfying.

Case study

The community health visitor teams were reorganised so that we could be more responsive to the needs of older people in the community. It meant that the existing teams were split up and new teams formed with a different mix of skills and different geographical areas to cover.

I understood the logic of the change and knew that it made sense. None of us was going to lose out financially from the move, and in fact I knew it would give me more opportunities to broaden my skills and experience.

At the same time I thought it was an extreme move. Why break up an effective team? Everyone in my team wanted to stay together. We had been working as a team for more than three years, knew each other's strong points, and were used to organising our own workload and supporting each other when needed. Part of the satisfaction I had from work was from being part of that team, so it was really hard to let go.

People who have change imposed on them may feel that they stand to lose a lot from the change, especially at first. This may be because the imposition of change undermines the control and choice individuals feel they have over their life.

The loss that someone experiences may not always be obvious to outsiders, especially when a change in one area of someone's life has a knock-on effect elsewhere.

Here is the health visitor again.

The area I used to cover in my job took me past a really nice park. I often used to take a few minutes' break to walk or just sit in the park – especially after a difficult visit. It helped me to relax and get things in perspective. I know it was a small thing, but I really didn't want to give it up. In the end, though, my new patch has its own attractions, including a supermarket – so I can do the shopping on my way home.

Activity

Consider these questions about the personal costs of change.

◆ What did you anticipate having to give up because of a change?

◆ How did you react to the thought of giving up these things?

◆ How did you deal with giving up those things in practice?

Sometimes the anticipation of loss is worse than the reality. We can adapt successfully to a new situation, given time. We look at adapting to change later in this chapter.

Change means increased workload

Change is often hard work. Not only do you have to keep some aspects of your personal and work life running, you also have to plan and organise the change, carry it out and adapt to the new situation.

The unexpected move

I wanted to move out of the city to live with my partner. So I had to find a new job nearer to him. I started to apply for jobs and landed the first one I applied for. It happened so quickly and at first my partner and I both had that sinking feeling: 'Oh no, what have I done?'

But there was no going back. Suddenly I had to organise getting my flat redecorated, letting it, and finding somewhere to store all my stuff, all while continuing to work, and help my previous employers find a replacement. I had a week between finishing my old job and starting the new. That's when I moved in with my partner.

It's been a hectic few months and I'm amazed I did it. Now I'm learning to live with my partner full time and find my way in the new job. I still don't feel my feet have quite touched the ground.

When your workplace is undergoing change the same is often true: the people affected by change have to continue to keep customers happy, while also dealing with the change, disruption and uncertainty.

If people are performing effectively in their work, then logically they should have little capacity to take on the work involved in a change that is not part of their normal responsibilities. Where change is additional to the usual workload, the pressure can mount.

Activity

What extra work was needed to make a change you've experienced recently?

◆ How far did the plans for change take into account the extra work required?

◆ How did you cope with this extra work?

◆ What would you suggest doing differently next time?

It is essential to acknowledge the extra work required to make change happen, and plan how to fit it in. If there is no recognition of the implications of change on workload, then the extra work required to bring about change can cause stress and burnout. The pressure people experience during change can reinforce resistance to change the next time.

Change means learning

Change involves learning new skills, new ways of doing things, new attitudes. It means acknowledging that current skills and expertise, behaviours and attitudes are no longer adequate or appropriate. How easy is it for people to give up their belief in their own competence?

Sometimes the need for learning new skills is recognised formally by an organisation when it builds training events into the change programme. You may start to learn something in a training course – the theory and basic principles, for instance – but it takes time and practice to build these into your usual methods of working.

At other times learning takes place informally as part of the process of adjusting to a new situation. For example, learning to work with new people, to use different procedures

The process of learning is not straightforward. A useful model shows that learning is a cycle – doing something, thinking about what happened and why, working out what to do differently next time and trying that out, and then starting the cycle again.

The learning cycle

Adapted from Kolb (1984)

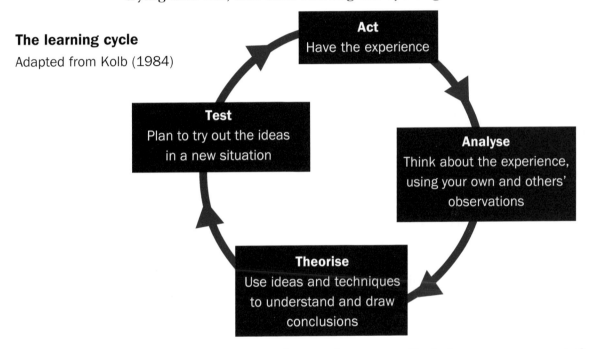

Act
Have the experience

Analyse
Think about the experience, using your own and others' observations

Theorise
Use ideas and techniques to understand and draw conclusions

Test
Plan to try out the ideas in a new situation

Learning is often deeply satisfying: you find that you can meet the challenges you face and build your experience and understanding. The ability to learn can give you confidence to deal with new change. But learning takes energy and application.

What can you do?

We have explored the concerns people have about change to help explain why most respond negatively when it is imposed on them. In the face of such concerns, you may be surprised that anyone ever changes. But concerns can be overcome – change does happen.

Before you can help other people to deal with change you need to overcome your own concerns.

Overcoming your concerns

Uncertainty

◆ Recognise that there is no real certainty; just a false sense of security.

◆ Find out about the change and why it is happening.

◆ Think through what the change means directly for you.

◆ Decide to take a positive view of the change.

◆ Set clear goals for yourself.

◆ Paint a clear positive picture of what the future will look like.

◆ Develop comprehensive plans with a step-by-step approach to the change.

◆ Keep yourself informed of developments.

Giving up something

◆ Identify what you will have to give up and acknowledge it.

◆ Consider ways of compensating for what you have to give up.

◆ Challenge exaggerations, assumptions and fears.

◆ List the opportunities and benefits for you in the change.

◆ Look forward – not back.

Increase in workload

◆ Identify the extra work required.

◆ Plan and make sure you have sufficient resources.

◆ Look after your well-being.

◆ Plan small rewards – things you enjoy – at key points during the change.

Learning

◆ Think about what you will need to learn and take up opportunities for training.

◆ Take time to review what is happening so you can learn from experience.

◆ It can also help to recognise that you are likely to go through a series of stages to adapt to change.

Adapting to change

Change affects people in different ways and your concerns about change will not be the same as those of your team members. But management experts tend to agree that people go through similar stages in order to come to terms with change.

Stages of adaptation

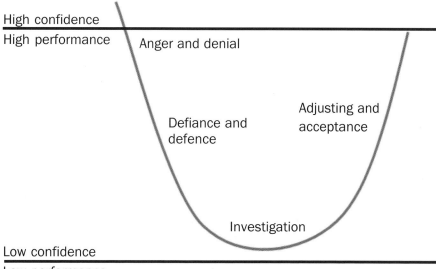

High confidence
High performance

Anger and denial

Adjusting and acceptance

Defiance and defence

Investigation

Low confidence
Low performance

As people go through these stages their confidence and performance are affected.

Anger and denial

The first stage may be shock and anger at the change and a refusal to believe it. Emotions are high, and people are unlikely to be receptive to new ideas or persuasion.

'I don't believe it.' 'It can't happen here.'

Defiance and defence

This stage is holding on to the current situation while rejecting the need for the change. There is an awareness of what will be lost, so resistance may be strong. At this stage confidence is plumeting.

'It won't work because...', 'I won't do it...' 'We can fight it...'

Investigation

This is the beginning of a realisation that the situation can't continue, and that the change is valid and will happen. Confidence and performance are likely to be rock bottom at this stage. It involves discarding the past and looking forward to explore the effects of the change.

'What will it mean for me?' 'How can I...? '

Adjusting and acceptance

Here, problems are solved, plans drawn up and implemented. It is the stage where the change occurs and the new situation is integrated into practice. Taking action and seeing how the change can happen help to build confidence and performance.

'To make this work, we'll need to...'

Activity

Do these stages make sense to you? Think about your reactions or the reactions of friends and colleagues, when they have faced a change. How far do you recognise the stages in adapting to a change?

People go through these stages at different speeds, perhaps depending on the nature of the change, their personal circumstances, the amount of loss they perceive, preferences for certainty or uncertainty and ability to look for opportunities and possibilities in a change. Some will adapt to a change quickly. Others will take longer, and may even seem to get stuck at different stages.

Managers and team leaders are no different from anyone else in their general responses to change. They too have to come to terms with the change. However managers have to adapt to change quickly if they are to lead their teams through the change.

It can be useful to recognise that we tend to go through these stages in adapting to change because it shows:

◆ We are not alone when we experience difficult emotions

◆ People can get through the stages successfully.

You may find it useful to take account of these stages as you come to terms with change.

In addition, these stages give us clues about how best to support people who are facing change, and how to manage the change so that they are able to adapt and accept it. For example, those at the anger and denial stage are unlikely to be ready to listen to any plans for the change. Indeed, you may find that such an approach only deepens a person's negative reaction. By responding sensitively to people you can help them to tackle their concerns about change and move through the stages.

Helping people to adapt

Helping people to adapt to change requires leadership skills. Here are some ideas for helping your team members move through move through each of the stages.

Anger and denial

Emotions are high and people are unlikely to be able or ready to listen. Focus on:

◆ Listening to individual concerns

◆ Acknowledging and understanding feelings

◆ Explaining why change is needed – the pressures for change

◆ Explaining what the change is designed to achieve.

Defiance and defence

People put forward objections and reject the change. There may be some flawed thinking. You need to listen carefully and counter objections. Confront false assumptions and irrational fears in a sensitive manner. Provide information about the change and be honest and open about what it will mean. It is important to start to talk about planning to show that the change is going to happen. Focus on:

◆ Listening to individuals

◆ Acknowledging losses and difficulties that concern individuals

◆ Challenging unfounded fears and misconceptions

◆ Putting down rumours

◆ Explaining the purpose and reasons for the change

- ◆ Exploring the benefits of the change for individuals
- ◆ Showing what the future will look like for the organisation and for individuals
- ◆ Mapping the process of making the change.

Investigation

As people start to explore what the change means for them you need to provide information and support, and encourage people to become involved in thinking through the implications of the change. Where possible, give people control over the change in their area. Focus on:

- ◆ Ensuring understanding
- ◆ Providing information
- ◆ Looking to the future rather than dwelling on the past
- ◆ Encouraging participation
- ◆ Supporting individuals
- ◆ Encouraging problem-solving
- ◆ Seeking views and feedback.

Adjustment and acceptance

Here, people are likely to be ready to become involved in planning and implementing the change. You need to show that you value their views and expertise and their work to implement the change. Focus on:

- ◆ Enquiring
- ◆ Encouraging involvement in planning and shaping the change
- ◆ Supporting decision-making
- ◆ Giving feedback on progress
- ◆ Celebrating early successes
- ◆ Looking to the future.

As you work with team members to adapt to change, bear in mind that some people may not be able to accept change. Even when they can see the benefits of change, they may not feel them personally. One of the reasons for this may be their personal circumstances.

People can choose whether or not to engage in change.

Helping people adapt to change requires frequent good communication and an ability to involve people in change. We look at these skills in Chapter 4 on Leadership.

Don't worry, Edna, I'll avoid using words containing the letter 't' until you find it

Look after yourself

As a manager or team leader you will be charged to lead the change with your team. To do this you must take care of yourself. This means:

◆ Taking a positive attitude to the change yourself.

◆ Avoiding stress by maintaining a good balance between your work and other aspects of your life.

A positive attitude

A positive attitude to change will help you to adapt to change quickly so that you are in a position to support your team. It requires:

◆ **Optimism** - Is your glass half empty or half full? An optimistic outlook is a bonus. How you think about a situation matters.

'Whether you think you can or you think you can't, you're probably right.'
Henry Ford

◆ **Self-confidence** - A belief that you have the personal resources and resilience to deal with whatever the future throws at you.

◆ **Courage** - An ability to look beyond the obvious negatives and face the reality of a change.

Radical change can mean restructuring, downsizing, redundancies and major disruption. The challenge for managers is to look beyond the negative effects of a change for the benefits and opportunities – all the actual and possible positive outcomes that can arise.

In my view the company made the right decision to restructure its operations. However, there were redundancies and the early stages of the change were not handled well, leaving people fearful that their job would be next and anxious about how they would manage with reduced numbers. Morale hit rock bottom. As I understood and agreed with the overall aims, I was able to see some opportunities. It would be worthwhile to build a strong team with a clear purpose – both for the team and for my future career options. I felt that the task was achievable, if only team members could be energised. That was the main challenge for me.

As a manager or team leader you can explore the benefits of a change from several perspectives: those of the organisation, team or work area, yourself and your staff.

Search for the benefits

Use the questions below to identify the opportunities and benefits of the change from all four perspectives.

Organisational perspective

◆ What is the change designed to achieve?

◆ What should it mean for the future success of the organisation as a whole?

Team perspective

◆ How is the team going to be affected by the change?

◆ How can it benefit the team? For example, will it provide:

❖ A redefined purpose and sense of direction?

❖ A richer mix of skills and expertise?

❖ Opportunities to work with other teams?

❖ Opportunities to learn directly from customers?

❖ A measurable contribution to the organisation?

Personal perspective

◆ What does the change mean for you personally and in terms of your career?

◆ How can you benefit from the change?

◆ What can you contribute both to the process of change and in the new changed situation?

◆ What can you learn?

Team member perspective

◆ How will team members benefit?

◆ Does the change mean opportunities for flexible working hours, improved conditions, training that increases individuals' employability, new working relationships, a clearer sense of purpose, potential for better rewards?

You may wish to explore the benefits of change with your team to help them see the positive side of change.

About stress

Pressure may be a natural part of working life that can help to improve performance. But too much pressure, especially over the long term, can lead to stress. There is no agreed definition of stress. But it can be described as the emotional, mental or physical strain that you may experience in situations which:

◆ You feel should not exist but that you cannot escape from.

◆ Put you under too much pressure for an extended period.

◆ Leave you short of time, resources, expertise, information, equipment, work or purpose.

Change may be another such situation, given that these factors are known to contribute to stress:

◆ Too much work in too little time

◆ Unrealistic demands

◆ Lack of control

◆ Fears over job security

◆ Uncertainty

◆ Confusion about roles

◆ Lack of communication and consultation.

Stress is a personal experience. The way you respond to the things that cause you stress depends on your personality and physiology.

Activity

See if you have any of these signs of long-term stress:

☐ anxiety   ☐ hostility or anger   ☐ exhaustion

☐ easily frustrated   ☐ irritability   ☐ tendency to blame others

☐ unable to make decisions ☐ poor concentrationsense of inadequacy

Stress can lead to health problems such as:

☐ headaches   ☐ gastric problems   ☐ raised blood pressure   ☐ insomnia

If you're concerned that you have signs of stress, talk to your doctor.

Organisations have an important role in helping their people to avoid or minimise stress during change. A supportive management and leadership culture will help. But the organisation should also provide training, support and counselling services.

In addition, you can develop personal ways of coping at work.

Tips for avoiding stress during change

Identify aspects of the change that are likely to cause you stress and see if you can minimise their effects by:

- Problem-solving
- Negotiating for resources with your managers
- Drawing on support available from colleagues and managers
- Managing your own time
- Avoiding working too long and too late
- Taking a lunch break
- Not taking work home
- Maintaining a balance between your work and personal life
- Taking a moment to have a light-hearted chat with people at work
- Avoiding negative thinking
- Being realistic and checking your assumptions.

A work-life balance

Most of us know what's good for us. We have a life outside work. We know that drinking, smoking, not getting enough exercise, eating junk food at the computer don't do us (or the computer) any good. But sometimes work seems to take over.

When I'm under a lot of pressure at work I usually work too late, sleep badly, grab a sandwich on the run and take too much comfort in a glass of wine at the end of the day. Work becomes a massive weight on my shoulders and I find it hard to think about anything else. It's like a downward spiral and a good recipe for stress.

To avoid stress and to keep a perspective on the place of work in your whole life it is useful to draw on your personal resources to keep a balance in your life.

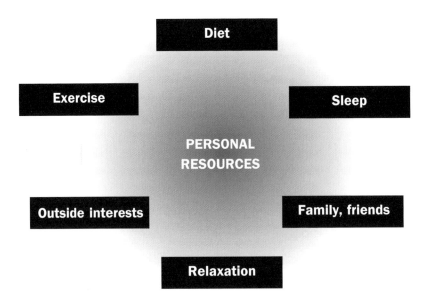

◆ Make a list of your personal resources in each of the headings above.

◆ Note things you enjoy doing, particularly the positive, healthy activities that you find refresh and invigorate you for the long term.

◆ From your list under each heading, note at least one action you can take during change in order to maintain a work-life balance.

◆ Think about people you can ask to help and support you, and what you would like them to do.

◆ Make sure your ideas are reasonable and realistic and you can achieve them.

◆ If you need advice on diet, sleep, exercise and relaxation, you could talk to your doctor or do some research on the Internet.

◆ To do some research online, go to a search engine, such as www.google.co.uk, and type in 'work-life balance'.

Find the balance

'Here are my resolutions for keeping a balance in my work. I talked to my family about this and we think I can do these things:

Family: Sit down with my family for dinner in evenings – 7.00 pm

Diet: Include fresh fruit at lunchtime

Exercise: Swimming with the children at weekends; walk part of the way to or from work three days a week

Sleep: No caffeine in the evening. Do a wind-down routine before going to bed – a warm shower works for me.'

Summary

◆ People often find change hard to cope with, and this may be because change means uncertainty, giving up something, more work and/or learning.

◆ People go through similar stages to come to terms with change: anger and denial, defiance and defence, investigation, adjusting and acceptance.

◆ As a manager or leader you need to go through the process of adapting to change, before you can help other people to adapt.

◆ You can use leadership skills, particularly communication and involving people, to help your team members come to terms with change.

◆ To adapt to change you need a positive attitude. One way to promote a positive attitude in yourself and in others is to identify the benefits of change.

◆ Change can cause stress, but stress is a personal experience, depending on your personality and physiology.

◆ Your organisation has a role in helping people to avoid stress. However, you can develop personal ways of coping at work.

◆ To avoid stress and to keep a perspective on the place of work in your whole life, it is useful to draw on your personal resources to keep a balance in your life.

◆ Your personal resources include interests outside work; friends, family; relaxation; exercise; diet; sleep.

3 Preparing for change

Introduction

This chapter focuses on four questions:

What needs to change?

This involves analysing your current situation and identifying priorities for change, using a SWOT analysis.

What do you want to achieve?

You have to be clear about the purpose and direction of change. In other words you need to picture the desired future situation and identify goals for change.

Where are you now?

It is important to look at your current situation in relation to the change, and consider the aspects that will work to promote change and those that will work against it. There are two key techniques:

◆ **Forcefield analysis** – examining the forces for and against the change

◆ **Stakeholder analysis** – anticipating the interests and expectations of the people who are going to be affected by the change.

How can you get started on change?

You know where you want to go and where you are now, and can start to see what needs to be done to bridge the gap.

The process of change is what you use to bridge the gap.

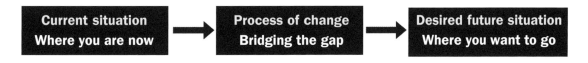

What needs to change?

At any time forces are acting on you that can trigger change. But which ones are the most important for you to respond to? Which will bring you most benefit? It is wise to keep an eye on the patterns and trends in the external environment, but it is also important to relate these to your current situation and circumstances.

It is impossible to talk about change unless you understand your starting point.

This allows you to prioritise the changes you need to make and gain maximum benefit from them.

A useful technique for looking at your current environment and identifying what needs to change is a SWOT analysis.

SWOT analysis

In a SWOT analysis you identify pressures for change in the external environment. These are the forces outside your sphere of influence. You then link these with the resources and capabilities at your disposal, enabling you to prioritise the changes you need to make.

SWOT stands for Strengths, Weaknesses, Opportunities, Threats. It can be used at any level in any type of organisation. You can also use it at a personal level. SWOT analysis is usually presented in a chart in which you list the relevant factors and show links between them.

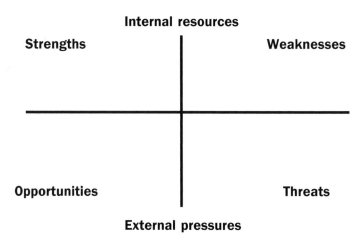

Opportunities and threats

These are the external pressures for change that may affect your organisation, your team or you personally, depending on the perspective used for the analysis.

External pressures at organisational level could include the PESTLE forces and forces in the market or industry or geographic area. External pressures at team level will include these as well as the pressures coming from elsewhere in the organisation – other teams, a change in strategy, a new boss. At a personal level, external pressures may come from the work you currently do, your team and organisation, as well as from factors in your personal life.

Strengths and weaknesses

These are the internal resources in your organisation, team or in you personally that will affect your ability to respond to the challenges you face. Resources available to your organisation or teams could come from a range of categories, like the following:

- **Products and services** – Do your products and services satisfy customer requirements? Are they profitable?

- **People** – Consider the skills and expertise available, the flexibility of working practices, working relationships, levels of motivation, willingness to take responsibility.

- **Culture** – How are things done in your organisation? Does everyone work together towards common goals? Are people protective of their own area of expertise and unwilling to share? Are people blamed for mistakes or are mistakes seen as opportunities to learn?

- **Systems** – The reward system, performance management system, quality management system, as well as IT systems such as information management and the Internet.

- **Work processes** – The process for taking and dispatching a customer order, the error-reporting process, the way work is assigned and logged.

- **Management style** – Is it bureaucratic or does it encourage decision-making at every level of the organisation? Is it formal or informal?

- ◆ **Availability of finance** – such as tight budgetary control, potential for capital investment.

- ◆ **Equipment, plant** – Is there extra capacity, is the plant up-to-date and well-maintained?

You may judge a resource to be a weakness or a strength, or both, depending on the circumstances.

A weakness or a threat?

A bureaucratic management style tends to mean that managers need to go through formal processes in order to make changes. This may mean that the organisation is inflexible and not able to respond quickly to new customer requirements. In this situation the management style is a weakness.

However, a bureaucratic management style may mean that the organisation is able to introduce a new organisational policy in a systematic manner. In this case the management style would count as a strength.

To carry out a SWOT analysis

1   Identify who the SWOT analysis is for – for you personally, for your team, department, unit, or organisation. This is the perspective you will take.

2   Make a list of the external pressures for change you are facing.

3   Start with the opportunities. These are pressures that you feel you could take advantage of or benefit from in some way.

4   Then list the threats. These are pressures that you have to respond to in order to remain competitive, legal and cost-effective

5   Now list the capabilities and resources you have. Assess each one as a strength or a weakness. Remember that a resource can be both a strength and a weakness depending on how it is to be used.

6   Review your list and highlight the opportunities and threats you think it most important to respond to. Use the following questions to identify key issues:

   ❖   What will happen if we don't respond to this?

   ❖   What will it mean if we do? Think about benefits to be gained, as well as the overall impact of responding.

It is likely that key opportunities and threats each link to some resources that can be viewed as strengths and some that can be viewed as weaknesses:

◆ A large number of strengths and few weaknesses indicate a good position to respond to the opportunity or threat.

◆ A large number of weaknesses and few strengths indicate that changes need to be made to meet the opportunity or threat.

A SWOT analysis gives a structured approach to thinking about what needs to change. It is clearly a matter of judgement, based on the subjective assessment of a situation. Your perception is likely to be different from another person's. For this reason it can be valuable to draw on the views of others when doing a SWOT analysis.

Hmm, we have one strength and three weaknesses. I say we run for it...

What do you want to achieve?

This is a simple question, but it is one that people often neglect when doing any kind of planning, never mind when planning change. This may be because the answer is not always easy to find, or because people fear that the answer will be wholly unrealistic given their current circumstances.

Goals must always be related to the current situation. You need to be able to map a route that will take you from where you are now to where you want to be.

So to identify what you want to achieve you really have to consider the two questions below:

You can start with either question.

◆ **Start with where you are now to keep your feet on the ground.** Identify the pressures for change and assess the resources at your disposal. Your goals will develop from the options you see open to you. This approach tends to tie your goals closely to your current situation.

◆ **Start with where you want to go to allow creativity and ambition**. You are free to take an imaginative leap and say what you really want to achieve. You may come up with some surprising answers; perhaps what you want to achieve is totally different from what you are currently working towards. But you still have to come down to earth and see where you are now and what is possible.

By answering both questions you can judge whether your goals for change are appropriate, given the current situation. If not, you may need to rethink your direction and priorities. If they are, you can finalise goals, starting with your vision for the future.

Creating a shared vision

The vision for the future looks beyond what you want to do, and focuses on what the change will bring - the desired future situation.

The people who initiate and lead change have to take others with them. So it is important to create a vision of the future that others can share. The vision needs to be desirable.

> The vision for change gives a shape to the future and focuses on the values and beliefs that underpin the change.

To identify the vision, think about the end result of change:

◆ State what you want to achieve - your purpose

◆ Paint a picture of what the future will look like

◆ Draw on abiding values or principles that are important and have meaning for the people affected by change.

The emphasis on values gives the rationale for the change - why it is being done. You can see why values are important by comparing the following statements:

We will cut our costs by 10%.	We will deliver the best-value products and services to customers.
We will train our staff in customer service and establish a performance management system that is customer-service oriented.	Our people will have the skills, resources, motivation and confidence to give customers exemplary service.
We will published policies on social responsibility and environmental policies.	Our business practices will show respect for the wider community and our environment.

The statements in the first column are about action, what will happen. They show intentions, but they are hardly inspiring.

The statements in the second column give a picture of what the future will be like. They are more inspiring and each could be a vision for change. They are concerned with values - to give exemplary service, to support staff, to show respect for the environment. They focus on benefits to people, not on systems and processes; and they have a long-term view. Most people would be able to support such statements.

A vision of the desired future should give everyone involved:

♦ A sense of purpose and direction, instead of fear and uncertainty

♦ Something that people can sign up to, endorse and support

♦ A touchstone for planning and action.

Of course, statements alone will not lead to support – at least not for long. It is important for those who lead the change to demonstrate their commitment to the vision with determined action, appropriate resources and a sustained interest in how the vision is to be achieved.

Developing a vision for change

If you develop a vision for change for a department or team it will have to be in line with the organisation's overall purpose, values and goals. These may be stated in the organisation's mission statement.

If the organisation doesn't have a mission statement, you can find out about its purpose and values in its publications and by considering its culture or the way the people in the organisation get things done.

In radical, top-down change, the organisation may renew its mission along with its vision. When you are faced with a new vision and mission, make sure that it is meaningful in your work area, creating one that is based on the new vision but is relevant to your team.

It is important to have a vision that other people can share and become excited about. Where possible, involve others in developing a vision. This helps people feel ownership and commitment to it.

Activity

For a change you want to implement, write a vision for the change, by considering the following questions:

♦ What is the purpose or aim in making the change?

♦ What benefits will the change bring to your work area?

♦ What values are involved?

♦ What will the changed future be like?

To answer this last question it may help to imagine what it will be like to work there or what it will be like to be a customer.

When you have written the vision, start to review it:

◆ Does the vision fit in with the organisation's purpose and values?

◆ How will the people affected by the change respond to the vision?

◆ How far do you think the vision will gain support?

◆ Will it help to motivate people to change?

A shared vision forms the basis for driving change forward.

From the vision can emerge the goals for change.

Goals for change

> The vision gives a rationale for the change – the *why*
>
> Goals show what needs to be done to achieve the vision

The goals begin to show what has to be done to make the vision a reality. Examples of goals for change are:

◆ To reduce costs by 10%.

◆ To train all staff in customer service.

◆ To establish a customer-oriented performance management system.

◆ To outsource a web design function.

They outline what needs to be done, but they don't go into detail or say how to achieve them.

Activity

Go back to the vision you created in the last activity, identify what needs to happen to achieve it. These are your goals. Are they realistic, given your current situation?

The vision and goals allow for action. But before you can move forward you need to consider where you are now in relation to the envisaged change.

Where are you now?

You know that change has to happen, and what you want to achieve. How do you move to your desired future situation? The approach will depend on the current situation – in particular the resources available and the willingness to change. Two techniques can help to assess this:

◆ Forcefield analysis

◆ Stakeholder analysis.

Forcefield analysis

In forcefield analysis you examine the forces in the current situation that can hinder or obstruct change, and those that can support or drive the change forward.

The forces for change may include goals and strategies for change, the people who are actively supporting it, resulting benefits to customers and to working practices, and problems with the current situation.

The forces against change include the costs incurred, such as training and additional resources; and resistance from staff and managers.

The strength of each force is assessed. If those for change are equal to those against, the result is equilibrium and nothing will change.

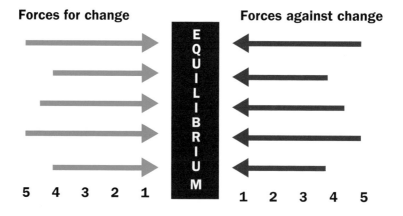

Forces for change　　　　　**Forces against change**

5　4　3　2　1　EQUILIBRIUM　1　2　3　4　5

The theory

Forcefield analysis was first developed by Kurt Lewin in 1951. The forces for change may be strong where there is senior management commitment and compelling external pressures, such as the need to conform to new legislation or to meet new customer requirements. If the forces for change outweigh those against then the change can be driven forward. But if the forces against are greater than those for change, then it may not be possible to carry out the change successfully, unless you can significantly influence the forces at work.

Influencing these forces is part of your role as a leader – you will want to build up the forces for change and decrease or minimise those against change.

Forcefield analysis helps you to see where you can most usefully focus your efforts. Consider the next case:

Branching out at an English language school

An English language school in the UK has an established reputation for its language teaching to young people from all over the world. The school principal wants to expand provision by providing business English courses to professional people. He proposes a new course structure – attended weekend courses backed up by an online classroom during the week which students log on to from their home base.

His first forcefield analysis looks like this:

Change: weekend and online courses for professionals

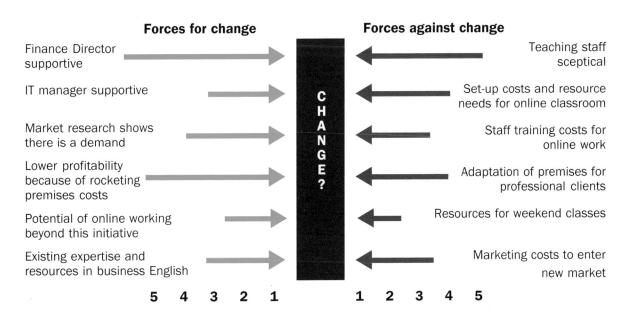

From this assessment the principal thinks that the forces for the change are greater than those that may resist it. However, he can't afford to be complacent.

He decides he needs to know more about the precise costs of introducing this change and the projected returns. He may not be able to reduce the costs by much but a clear picture of what the school can hope to gain will help his case.

He must also find ways to turn round the scepticism of staff. He realises he needs his teaching staff to be enthusiastic not negative.

To carry out a forcefield analysis

1 Write down your main goal, your desired future situation.

2 Make a list of all the forces for the change – the external pressures driving change, peole who actively support the change and so on.

3 Make a list of all the forces that are against the change – costs, barriers and obstacles, including people who are likely to resist the change.

4 Assess the strength of each force, its influence or power. Give each a score from 1 to 5, where 1 is weak and 5 is very strong.

5 To make this assessment use your judgement, based on your knowledge and experience. You could discuss this assessment with experienced colleagues and draw on their judgement as well.

6 Draw your results in the form of a forcefield diagram, showing each force as an arrow whose tail represents its strength.

7 Examine what the diagram tells you. Use the following questions to help:

◆ Can you make the change in the current situation?

◆ Which forces can you influence?

◆ How can you strengthen support for the change?

◆ Can you add to the positive forces?

◆ How can you minimise the effects of the forces against the change?

People are among the forces you consider in a forcefield analysis. You need to have people on your side so it is worth considering their position and perspective in more detail.

Stakeholder analysis

An analysis of stakeholders will help you build an understanding of the people affected by a change. An organisation's stakeholders are all the people and groups that have a stake or interest in the organisation. A commercial organisation may have the following stakeholders:

The organisation's stakeholders

All these stakeholders have their own concerns about change.

> Stakeholder analysis is a technique for examining the relative power and influence of each stakeholder group, the impact of change on them, their likely response and expectations from the change.

You can choose a perspective from which to analyse stakeholders, depending on the type of change you are seeking to lead. For example, the people leading radical change that will affect the whole organisation will examine the organisation's stakeholders. If you are leading a change in your team you can analyse the team's stakeholders.

The first step in stakeholder analysis is to identify your stakeholders.

Identify the team's stakeholders

These are the people and groups who have an interest in or are affected by the work you and your team do. They will include:

◆ **Customers** - the people to whom you provide products or services. They may be:

❖ Internal customers, i.e. working in the same organisation as you (if you give your manager a report, he or she is your customer) and

❖ External customers (the people outside the organisation who buy or use its products or services).

◆ **Suppliers** - the people and groups that supply you with the products and services you need to do your work. Again, they may be internal (an IT expert in your organisation provides you with computer support) or external (the organisation that provides your team with stationery and office equipment).

◆ **Your managers and other teams** in the organisation - these may also be your customers and suppliers depending on whether they receive or supply products and services to the team.

◆ **Team members** - the people who carry out the work of your team and generate its products and services. They have a stake in how the team operates and in their role and opportunities as team members.

You may also want to include owners and shareholders, regulators, such as those concerned with health and safety, local community groups that have an interest in your team's activities.

Activity

Make a list of your key stakeholders and group them into categories such as those listed above. You can do this from your team's perspective or from an individual standpoint.

When you have listed your stakeholders continue the analysis by considering the change from their point of view.

Case study

I am a contact centre manager, and we are planning to introduce new working practices and a performance management system to address our customers' requirements and improve efficiency. My analysis of key stakeholders is that:

◆ Owners or shareholders expect higher profits through increased efficiency.

◆ Senior managers expect a smooth transition with minimum costs and disruption to the service provided to customers.

◆ Customers want a better level of service, shorter waiting times, an order tracking service, the ability to speak to a real person who understands the product and customers' needs.

◆ Team members are concerned about their jobs and working conditions. They want to know what the change will mean for their own work, both while the change is underway and afterwards when it is in place.

In practice the managers have the most power in driving the change – senior managers have share options in the company so they stand to gain if the change delivers expected increases in productivity.

Customers and shareholders have hardly any power to influence the change process, even though the change is designed to meet customers' needs and the plan is to improve profitability to benefit shareholders.

In theory team members have little power, but they are most directly affected by the changes, and can influence the way it is implemented. They have power to obstruct or delay successful implementation. The new performance-related reward scheme will benefit the high achievers, but those who are less motivated or are not so skilled will struggle to take home the same pay.

Such an analysis will show you who is likely to support the change, who is likely to resist it and why. It highlights the range of interests that may be concerned with the change and who has most power to affect its formulation and outcome.

Activity

For a change you want to introduce in your team, analyse your team's stakeholders to identify:

◆   Their interests, concerns and expectations in the change

◆   Who is most likely to gain and lose from it

◆   Their level of power and influence.

When you have done this, identify who is likely to support the change and who may resist it.

Think about what you can do to overcome resistance and build on support.

Your analysis is based on your judgement and experience. This can be valuable, but you shouldn't rely on it. Test your assumptions and conclusions by talking to people and finding out what they say their concerns are. Be prepared to modify your analysis as you gain more information.

Your assessment of what different people expect from the change process and the resulting changed situation can help you plan how to satisfy the different, and sometimes competing, interests and plan your approach to overcome resistance and build on support.

As a starting point, make sure that you address stakeholders' particular interests in the way you communicate with them. Appealing to the interests and viewpoints of others is key to any form of negotiation or persuasion.

Look at the following ways of overcoming resistance and building support, and identify those that you will use when you need to prepare for change.

Ways of overcoming resistance and building support

Be clear about the need for change

◆ Explain why change is needed – the forces that are leading to change and why the current situation is not sustainable.

◆ Provide a vision of the desired future situation that incorporates values that most people can endorse and support.

◆ Show that the vision has active support from senior managers.

◆ Show personal enthusiasm and commitment to the change.

Explore implications of change

◆ Involve people in exploring the implications of change.

◆ Focus on the benefits of the change for the organisation, team and individual.

◆ Be clear about the scope for individuals to influence the change or the plans for change.

◆ Identify what implementing the change will mean.

Respond to emotions

◆ Acknowledge and accept fears and concerns.

◆ Understand what people feel they will have to give up.

◆ Challenge misconceptions and rumours.

◆ Work with individuals who find it difficult to accept the change.

Focus on the task ahead

◆ Encourage people to become involved in planning and implementing the change.

◆ Where possible, give people tasks that allow them to address their concerns.

◆ Look for early successes.

How can you get started?

You know change is needed, you know what you want to achieve, you know the forces and interests that are operating in your current situation. The next stage is to create momentum for the change and mobilise energy to make the change happen.

A well-known three-phase model of the change process is this:

The theory

The three-phase model was described by Kurt Lewin, who developed forcefield analysis. His suggestion was that to stimulate change the forces operating in a stable situation need to be shaken up.

This model tends to assume that change is finite and that stability needs to be established afterwards. We know that change is not an occasional event, but a constant. There may be a continuous cycle of change or it may be open-ended. However, the model is still useful in highlighting the need to unfreeze a stable or comfortable situation.

The following gives some suggestions for action at each phase of the change process.

Unfreeze	Recognising the need for change
	Identifying what needs to change
	Building support for the vision of the future
	Reducing forces obstructing change
	Strengthening forces supporting and driving change
Move	Setting goals, objectives and standards to achieve the vision
	Planning action
	Implementing
	Integrating new systems, policies and methods to support the new situation and new behaviours
Refreeze	Evaluating the change process and outcomes
	Learning from the process

Two key skills throughout the process are **communication** and **involving people**. The next chapter is about leadership and has a focus on these two skills.

Summary

◆ A SWOT analysis enables you to examine your current situation. It involves identifying external pressures for change and relating them to the resources and capabilities at your disposal.

◆ To set goals for change you need to be clear about where you are now, and where you want to go.

◆ The vision for change gives a shape to the future and focuses on the values and beliefs that underpin the change. The goals show what needs to be done to achieve the vision.

◆ A shared vision provides the basis for driving change forward.

◆ To determine how to make the change happen, use the following techniques:

  ❖ Forcefield analysis examines the supporting and opposing forces around change.

  ❖ Stakeholder analysis looks at the interests of those affected by change to identify who will support or oppose change and why.

◆ A three-phase model of the change process suggests ways of getting the change underway. It is: unfreeze, move, refreeze.

4 Leadership

Introduction

As a leader of change your aim is to help people adapt to change and contribute positively to the new situation in order to achieve the desired future.

Open two-way communication and involving people are the main building blocks of leading through change. But these two skills must be supported by key leadership qualities. With these three you can:

◆ Show you respect your people

◆ Build trust in the change

and in this way

◆ Work with your team to make change a success.

The role of leadership in change

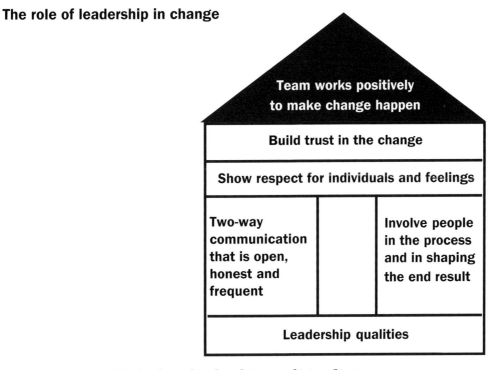

We look at leadership qualities first.

Leadership qualities

Leadership attitudes

There are two extremes of attitude for managing and leading people: the stick approach and the carrot approach. Whether you tend towards the stick end of the spectrum or the carrot end will depend largely on your view of basic human nature.

Stick	Carrot

Leadership attitudes to people: the stick – carrot spectrum

The stick approach

Managers or leaders who are at this end of the stick-carrot spectrum believe in sanctions and close supervision as the way to get people to perform. They think that people are basically lazy and don't like work, and that they will avoid responsibility. They think people have little potential for development.

The carrot approach

Managers or leaders at this end of the spectrum believe in creating conditions that enable people to be motivated and gain a sense of achievement from work. They believe that most people like to work. They think people will take responsibility and direct their own work, particularly when their contribution is valued and respected. They think people have potential and will rise to a challenge if they are given the opportunity.

The theory

Douglas McGregor – management theorist and researcher – described two extremes in management attitudes as long ago as 1967 in his well-known work, *The Human Side of Enterprise*. He identified the two attitudes as Theory X (similar to the stick approach) and Theory Y (similar to the carrot approach).

Think about your own attitudes to people.

Where would you place yourself on the stick–carrot spectrum?

The stick and carrot approaches are, of course a simplification. But attitudes influence behaviour, and in the same way your position on the spectrum will affect your management or leadership style.

◆ If you tend towards the stick end of the spectrum, you are in a management tradition that emphasises direction and control. You tend to have low expectations of your people.

◆ If you tend towards the carrot end, you are moving towards a leadership approach, which aims to empower people. You tend to have high expectations of your people.

A manager's attitudes and expectations will usually be reflected in the attitudes of his or her staff. So if you encourage people and value the contribution they make, your staff are likely to feel appreciated and willing to put effort and energy into their work. But if you feel people have little to contribute, they will recognise your lack of confidence in them and be reluctant to engage with their work.

A person's attitudes can become a self-fulfilling prophesy.

To lead people through change you want people on your side, enthusiastic and committed to working towards a shared vision and goals for the future.

If you find yourself near the stick end of the spectrum your ability to lead change is likely to be weak. However you can shift your attitudes towards the carrot end.

You already know it can be difficult to change, and particularly hard to change attitudes. However, you also know that change does happen and is possible. Undergoing this kind of change will give you valuable experience which you can use to help other people adapt to change. Draw on the techniques and ideas in this book. One technique that may be particularly useful is to develop your self-awareness by challenging your assumptions.

Challenging assumptions

Developing an understanding of what makes you and other people tick is important when leading people through change, so that you can deal with individuals sensitively, honestly and without preconceptions.

As a leader you can choose to adopt a thoughtful, enquiring approach to your own actions, and the attitudes and beliefs that influence them, by challenging your assumptions. Such an approach helps you develop your own self-awareness and keep an open mind.

An assumption is something you believe to be true, even though you don't have any proof that it is. We draw on different sources of information, such as experience, observation and knowledge of a situation, to form assumptions. From these assumptions we draw conclusions, plan and take action. The results of our action often reinforce our assumptions.

We have to make assumptions in order to operate. For example, yesterday the car was working fine. So today I assume that the car will start, which allows me to plan to drive to my business meeting. This is a reasonable assumption. It works, most of the time.

Making assumptions

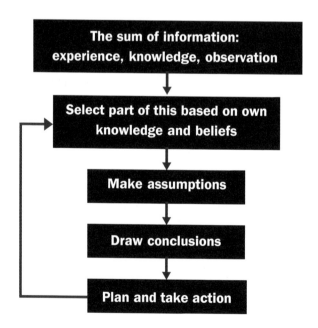

However, we may draw on incomplete or inaccurate information, or filter it because of our beliefs and attitudes. This can make our assumptions unsafe. Consider the story below.

False assumptions

Petra noticed that James was not contributing ideas to team discussions on the office relocation. He simply said it was going to be difficult to get to the new site. He seemed surly and uncooperative and had been late for work several times in the past week, without explanation. Petra had always found James to be rather inflexible about working conditions, and concluded that he was resistant to the change. She was irritated by this because she felt the rest of the team was becoming enthusiastic about the move. She decided not to include him in the relocation team. A few days later James asked to see her. He apologised for his recent lateness, explained that his disabled wife had become seriously ill and requested some flexibility in his working hours.

It is easy to become fixed in patterns of thinking and make false assumptions. These can undermine your credibility as a leader. One way of challenging assumptions is to reflect on events.

Challenging assumptions

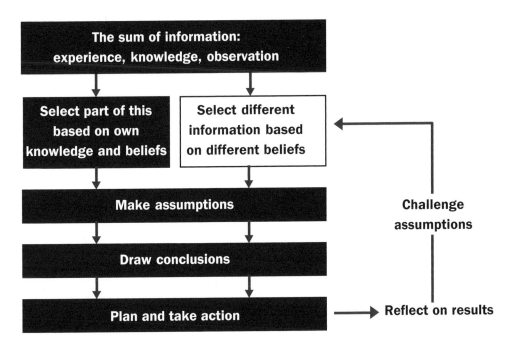

Reflecting on the situation, Petra had to admit that she hadn't known of James's personal circumstances. She realised that she had been jumping to conclusions about James's attitudes, and decided she ought to make time to get to know her team.

Reflecting on events can help you gain a deeper understanding of your behaviour and improve your self-awareness. Take time to step back from an event and review it, thinking about what happened, why it happened, what went well and what you could do differently next time. You don't have to do this just for events that you feel you could have handled better. It is equally valuable to do this for events that you feel went well.

You can use the following set of questions to help you to reflect on events.

Reflecting on events

Describe the event

◆ What were your intentions?

◆ What did you say and do?

◆ What happened as a result of your behaviour?

◆ How did you feel about it?

◆ How do you think other people felt? What evidence do you have for the way they felt?

◆ What knowledge, attitudes, beliefs and emotions influenced your behaviour?

◆ What if anything would you do differently next time?

◆ What can you learn from the event?

Be a role model for change

Your attitudes and behaviour have an impact on your team members. They will be watching you and take you as a role model.

Activity

Think about how you would want a role model for change to behave, then create a list of qualities you would value in a role model. As a starting point read the following suggestions, tick the ones you agree with, and add to the list.

- ☐ Enthusiasm and motivation
- ☐ A positive attitude to change
- ☐ Commitment to a shared vision for the future
- ☐ Concern and support for people
- ☐ Maintaining a focus on what matters.e.g. meeting customer requirements
- ☐ Honesty and integrity
- ☐ Even-handed and level-headed
- ☐ Willingness to learn
- ☐ Able to deal with setbacks

You will demonstrate your qualities as a role model all the time in the way you behave and in the way you communicate.

Communication

- ◆ How can you inspire your team to share your vision of a changed future?

- ◆ How can you understand and respond to your team's concerns?

- ◆ How can you encourage team members to help make change work for them?

To do all these, and so lead your team effectively you need to communicate – and communicate well.

We all communicate, all the time, and often without giving it any thought. But communication often fails: the message gets lost, distorted, misunderstood or misrepresented, leading to wasted time, friction, resistance and conflict. When you are leading change you certainly don't need to create these sorts of barriers. You should be able to use communication as a tool to make change happen.

So take it apart and plan to use it purposefully.

The communication process

Good communication is about building understanding.

Good communication is open. This means that it is not constrained or limited because of the power or authority of either party. In open communication people talk freely, expressing their thoughts, ideas and feelings without fear of ridicule or blame. You have a key role in encouraging open communication.

Good communication is an exchange between a sender and receiver. It is two-way. The sender sends a message to a receiver and the receiver sends feedback which indicates how far the message is understood.

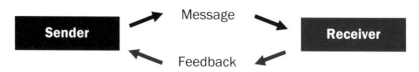

In contrast an announcement is one-way, with no opportunity for the receiver to give feedback directly to the sender. So it doesn't amount to good communication.

The two-way nature of communication means that leaders must pay attention to their role in:

◆ Sending messages

◆ Listening

◆ Asking questions.

Sending messages

In sending messages you have to think not just about your role and the content of your communication, but also about who is going to receive these messages and how they will be interpreted and understood. Six planning questions can help.

Six planning questions

1 What do you want to **achieve**?

2 What do the **people** receiving your message need?

3 What's the best **method** to use?

4 What does the **message** contain?

5 When's the best **time** to communicate?

6 How do you get any **feedback** you need?

We look at what to consider in answering each question.

What do you want to achieve?

When you're dealing with change, your aim in communicating could be any of the following:

◆ Inform

◆ Influence or persuade

◆ Motivate

◆ Encourage

◆ Seek commitment

- ◆ Instruct or direct

- ◆ Ask for feedback

- ◆ Ask for information

- ◆ Investigate or find out

- ◆ Gather opinions and views

- ◆ Seek agreement.

Each of these different aims influences what you communicate and how you do it. So it is important to be clear about your purpose and reason for communicating.

Notice that in order to achieve these different aims the sender needs to elicit a particular response from the person or people receiving the message. This means that you must tailor your communication to the recipients.

What do the people receiving the message need?

Communications often fail because the sender doesn't appreciate the importance of recipients. The success of communications depends on considering their requirements and adapting the communication to their needs.

Think about the recipients and their:

- ◆ **Interests and concerns in the subject**. Think about how far it affects them, their likely perspective and what they wish to gain from it. It may be important to focus on the aspects that will particularly interest them.

- ◆ **Possible emotional responses**. If the message is likely to create anxiety, you may take particular care over the tone and method you use. Think about how to enable people to give feedback and how you can listen to and respond to this.

- ◆ **Level of understanding and knowledge of the subject**. If people have little knowledge, you may have to provide background information to reinforce your message. Will they understand any jargon or technical terms?

- ◆ **Preferences**. If you know your manager dislikes long emails, keep them short.

In analysing recipients' needs take care not to jump to conclusions or make wrong assumptions about your recipients. You could ask them, for example, what they know about a subject, but you can also draw on your experience and observations of them.

It is worth checking your assumptions as you send the message by asking for feedback. If this indicates you are failing to achieve your aims, you can often modify your message.

Know your audience's needs

New contact centre equipment was installed in the new office, and the technical services team had to introduce it to operators and their team leaders before training started. At first the plan was to do this on a team basis, but when the technical services team talked to operators and team leaders it found that they each had different concerns. The operators wanted to know how to use the new equipment, and how soon they would get used to it. The team leaders wanted to know about its functionality and how it would enhance their ability to monitor performance. The service team designed different sessions for each audience.

> The most important of the six planning questions is 'What do the people receiving the message need?'

What's the best method to use?

There is a wide range of options:

Spoken: one-to-one discussions or meetings, team briefings, group meetings, presentations

◆ may take place face-to-face, over the telephone, with web-cam or video conferencing

Written: emails, letters, reports, briefing papers, notices, text messages

◆ may be sent by the Internet or intranet, fax, tele-phone or by post

Visual: charts, graphs, diagrams, pictures, slide shows, can reinforce both spoken and written communications

◆ body language, such as gestures, expressions and eye contact, can affect the way a message is received.

Normal work was interrupted over the rest of the day, and I talked it over with quite a few team members. The next day we met again, and I was able to summarise what I'd discussed with people and answer more questions. I explained that I didn't know the answer to all the questions. The second meeting was fraught, but at least people had had time to think about what was going to happen and we could begin to deal with some of the issues.

How do you get any feedback you need?

'I left a message...'

'I sent an email...'

Unless you get a response to your message you can't know whether it has been received, never mind whether it has been understood as intended. When communications use technology or written communications, you may need to ask for feedback to your messages:

'Please reply to this email to acknowledge receipt.'

'Please call me early next week to discuss this.'

'Call me back to let me know you've got this message.'

Feedback in spoken conversation is often automatic. The way someone responds – the words spoken and the body language – may be all that's needed to indicate how far a message is received and understood. However, you can also ask questions to check understanding.

Activity

Use the six planning questions to plan an important message you need to send.

◆ What do you want to achieve?

◆ What do the people receiving your message need?

◆ What's the best method to use?

◆ What does the message contain?

◆ When's the best time to communicate?

◆ How do you get any feedback you need?

After you have made the communication, review your success. How useful did you find these planning questions?

Although you are unlikely to have the time to plan any but the most important communications in detail, you can use the questions to pause and think through what you want to communicate and how best to do so, rather than plunging straight in regardless of the consequences. It can be particularly useful to consider the first two questions when you are speaking to people.

Listening and using questions

One of the aims of communicating during change is to encourage your team members to:

◆ Express their feelings and responses to change

◆ Give their views and opinions

◆ Explore what change may mean to them

◆ Adapt to change

◆ Become committed to change.

This means listening carefully to make sure that you hear and understand what is being said and using questions to encourage people to express their feelings and opinions.

Listening

Real listening shows an interest in the speaker and a desire to understand his or her opinions and feelings.

The willingness to put yourself in someone else's shoes is known as empathy. It doesn't mean agreeing, but it does mean acknowledging and accepting what someone says:

'I can see that it must be frustrating for you that the changes have disrupted your project.'

'I know it's hard working in these conditions. We are on course to move to the new building in 15 days, and counting.'

'I understand why you are complaining about the system when you keep getting error messages.'

Check your listening skills by practising listening to someone. Ask a friend to talk to you about something – a holiday, a problem at work, for example – and concentrate on listening carefully to what he or she says.

Afterwards discuss what happened with your friend:

◆ Did your friend think you were genuinely listening? '

◆ Or did he or she think you were just going through the motions of listening?

◆ How did he or she feel?

◆ What did you do that showed you were listening?

◆ What did you do that suggested that you weren't listening?

◆ How did you feel about the exercise?

◆ Did you find it easy to listen?

When someone genuinely listens, the speaker tends to feel respected and valued. Most people can tell when someone is or isn't listening.

'I wanted to explain my concerns about the change. My team leader invited me in, sat me down and said he wanted to hear. But his eyes kept straying to some papers on his desk, and I was sure I was interrupting him. I just dried up. I found it very awkward.'

But listening is surprisingly hard work to do well. It requires you to give your full attention to the person speaking.

Use the guidelines here to improve your listening.

How to listen

◆ Find an appropriate place to talk privately, using comfortable seating arranged informally

◆ Put other thoughts out of your head

◆ Give your full attention to the speaker

◆ Be alert to feelings as well as to the words spoken

◆ Don't interrupt the speaker's flow with your own ideas

◆ Encourage the speaker to continue to talk by using verbal cues, such as 'Go on...', 'I see...', 'Mmm...'. This shows that you are with the speaker and want to know more.

◆ Show your interest with appropriate body language. a relaxed posture, occasional eye contact, facial expressions that match what the person is saying.

◆ Suspend your own judgement while you are listening.

◆ Acknowledge and accept what the person is saying – you don't have to agree.

◆ Show you have understood, by checking and summarising: 'So, what you're saying is...?'

◆ Use appropriate questions to help the speaker focus his or her thoughts.

Activity

Go through the list of techniques above and tick those that you tend to use when you are listening.

Make a note of the ones you think you may find useful in future.

Asking questions

The type of question you use, whether your purpose is to encourage someone to express themselves or to find out information, will affect the response you receive. There are three basic types:

Closed questions

For example: '*Do you understand...?*' '*Do you share the vision?*'

They can be answered with 'yes', 'no' or 'don't know.'

They ask for specific information, which can be useful for clarifying something, but they can close down a dialogue.

Open questions

For example: '*How do you feel about ...?*' '*Why do you think change is needed?*' '*What are your goals?*'

They usually start with 'what', 'how' and 'why'. Alternatively you could use 'Tell me ...' to invite someone to speak.

These encourage someone to open up and express their view in the way they choose. They can be used to probe or clarify someone's emotions and beliefs.

But bear in mind that questions starting with 'Why...?' can seem to be asking for justification.

Leading questions

For example: '*You do share our vision for the future, don't you?*' '*You won't want to try it, will you?*'

These suggest the answer the questioner is expecting or wants to hear. These are best avoided because they can be seen as bullying.

Skilful listening and questioning are both important when you are seeking to engage and involve people in the change.

Involving people

You can involve people right at the start of change, although the nature of involvement depends on the type of change.

◆ When you are initiating change in your work area you can involve your team members in identifying the external factors that trigger the need for change, and then in drawing up a shared vision and goals. This puts team members in a good position to become involved in planning the implementation.

◆ In radical top-down change, the senior management team make decisions and impose change without consultation. In these situations team members have no role in shaping the change. However they do have a role in shaping the consequences of change in their work area. You can involve team members by communicating the need for change as early as possible, helping them to understand the change and what it means for them. This helps people adapt to the change, it also gives them the information and background knowledge they need to contribute to decision-making and planning to make the change in their work area.

> Involve people affected by change in shaping the change. When this is not possible involve them in shaping the consequences of change.

The benefits

How does it feel when you're not involved in a change that is going to affect you? You may feel that:

◆ You've lost control over your life.

◆ Change is happening *to* you not *by* you.

◆ Your skills, experience and expertise are not valued.

◆ You are expected to shelve your own judgement and just do what you're told.

◆ You don't want the change to be a success – so your overall response is hostile.

In contrast, what is it like when you are involved in a change?

Involvement is usually lively, to say the least. People have to question their assumptions and the usual way of doing things. Disagreements are expressed and explored, and these may lead to conflict.

With involvement you have some degree of control and your scope for choice becomes clear. When you are involved you may feel:

◆ Interested and engaged

◆ Respected and valued for your skills, expertise and experience.

◆ Challenged and stimulated

◆ Motivated and committed to the change.

> By involving people in change you are encouraging them to invest in the change, to have some role in shaping the 'desired future situation', to take some control. This gives people a real stake in the change: they want to see it work.

Commitment and motivation are just some of the benefits of involvement. It also has these benefits:

◆ An improved quality of decision-making – through the pooling of different skills, expertise, experience and perspectives

◆ Greater understanding among people

◆ Less management control is needed – people understand what needs to be done and why and are better placed to take responsibility and monitor progress themselves.

Encouraging other people to participate takes time and effort, especially at the planning stage, but involving your team members in change, benefits you as the person managing and leading the change, team members and the process. However, involving people doesn't happen automatically or naturally, especially if it is not an established tradition. You may have to knock down barriers to participation.

Barriers to participation

Key barriers to participation include:

◆ The attitudes and actions of managers

◆ The expectations of team members.

If you usually adopt a directive style and rarely consult, your staff may be suspicious or unwilling to contribute when you suddenly change your approach. They may see decision-making as your role and responsibility, and think that you are seeking to offload your duties onto them. So they will probably want to know what's in it for them.

This reticence will be stronger if there are low levels of motivation among team members, and if the culture in your work area doesn't show respect for people. Participation may not be easy in a culture where people 'watch their backs' for fear of being blamed, or in a culture that is 'them' the managers and 'us' the workers.

Encouraging participation

You can't force people to become engaged in change, and you may have no power to alter the overall conditions in your organisation. But you can use leadership skills in four key areas to create an atmosphere between yourself and your team that encourages participation:

◆ Get to know the concerns of your team members

◆ Focus attention and effort on the task

◆ Adapt your leadership style

◆ Support your staff.

Get to know team members' concerns

When you know what matters to your team members, you can provide specific support that helps them address their concerns.

But how well do you know your team members? You can find out about their concerns and interests when they are facing change by communicating openly, in both formal and informal situations, in group meetings and one-to-one discussions.

Your main purpose in communicating may be to inform your team of a change, but you can take the opportunity to ask for the views of your team members, and really listen to what they say. If the level of trust between you and your team members is low, it is up to you to take the risk and trust them with some personal information about yourself. For example, you could reveal something of your own concerns about change in general and perhaps this change in particular.

Change gives plenty of opportunities for communicating formally – keeping people informed is a crucial part of your role. But don't forget informal communications, especially conversation.

Make conversation

Conversation doesn't need a purpose and isn't planned. It just needs two or more people. There are few rules, beyond courtesy and consideration. It can take place anywhere: the walk to the car park, by the coffee machine, at the printer. Topics can range far and wide, from work to play, there may be strange leaps from one topic to another, talk about nothing in particular, jokes, inconsequential gossip and light-hearted comments. It can be broken off or interrupted and it doesn't matter. In conversation you glimpse into aspects of another person's life and personality and in turn you reveal something of yourself. You find you share some opinions and have differences in other areas.

Conversation is valuable for all sorts of reasons:

◆ It can relieve tension, awkwardness or embarrassment.

◆ It helps people get to know each other in a natural, unforced way.

◆ It allows people to choose how much to reveal of themselves – they may remain guarded until they know more about each other.

◆ It builds trust and confidence gradually: people can feel their way, choosing safe topics at first, until they judge they can risk revealing more.

Like good communication, conversation can build understanding.

Focus on the task

One of the most important ways of involving people is to focus people's attention on what needs to be done and use positive action towards the change to replace the negative emotional responses they may have, such as fear, anxiety and confusion.

With an understanding both of what concerns people and what needs to be done to plan and implement change you can allocate tasks that help to address their concerns.

You can also look for tasks that will deliver some success early on in the process.

Abel, a member of a sales team was usually a high performer. He worked hard for his individual customers and achieved results and consequently good rewards. The change meant moving to a customer relationship team, so that customers has direct access to the expertise they need. Abel was struggling to see how he would benefit from this new team approach. His manager, recognising Abel's concern, invited him to work with others to design the reward system for the team.

Grace was the team leader of a new team, which included some home workers, as well as people from different parts of the company. The team members were anxious about how the team would work. Grace brought all the team members together for a team meeting to discuss, agree and write the team contract.

The meeting helped team members to get to know each other. But, more important was the fact that it also produced an agreed team contract. This showed everyone that it was possible for them to work together as a team.

Match people to tasks

◆ Identify processes, procedures, and policies that need to be addressed to make the change work.

◆ Choose tasks that will contribute to the change and deliver success quickly.

◆ Be clear about what skills are required and what people have currently, and arrange training opportunities.

◆ Find out what concerns people have, and where possible match people to tasks that will help them address those concerns.

◆ Invite people who are reluctant to get involved to give it a try.

◆ Keep everyone informed and up-to-date about who is doing what.

◆ Be clear about your expectations – how people need to act and how performance will be measured.

◆ Choose an appropriate leadership style.

◆ Celebrate success.

Use positive action to help people see a way through their resistance to change.

Leadership style

Leadership style is the way the leader of a team makes decisions, defines tasks, sets objectives, monitors and supervises tasks.

You can choose an appropriate leadership style to increase involvement and participation.

A useful way of categorising leadership styles is by the level of control a leader retains, compared to the level of control experienced by team members. For the leader, levels of trust and control are related. As trust increases the leader feels able to relinquish more direct control, and pass responsibility, ownership and control to individual team members.

There are four basic leadership styles.

Leadership styles

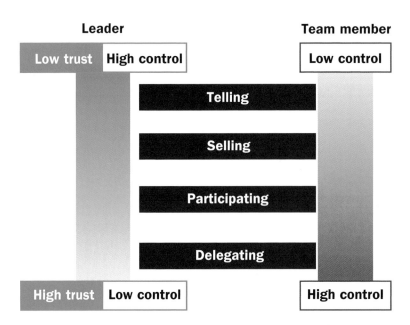

Telling – a directive style that involves giving specific instructions and providing close monitoring and supervision:

'This is what we need to do...'

'This is how we're going to do it...'

Selling – explaining the reasons why a task needs to be done and giving plenty of support in order to increase commitment:

'This is what we need to do because...'

'We're going to do it this way so that we can...'

Participating – a consultative style which requires a lot of communication between manager and team members, so that team members understand the issues involved and can contribute to planning and controlling their work within known constraints.

'Let's decide what we need to do...'

'What do you think...?'

'Let's agree on how we're going to do it...'

Delegating – the manager gives responsibility and authority to team members to plan and implement specific parts of their work.

'Tell me what you're going to do to achieve our goals...'

'Tell me how you're going to do it...'

Activity

Which of these styles do you feel most comfortable using?

When do you vary your style?

Studies carried out by management researchers and theorists suggest that each of these styles may be appropriate in particular situations. There isn't one preferred or recommended style of leadership. However, people are more likely to be motivated and engaged when they feel they have some control and responsibility for the work they are doing. So your aim will be to relinquish control to others where possible.

Effective leaders adapt their style according to two factors:

◆ **The nature of the task**

The scope and context of the task, the information and resources needed, the timescale, will influence the style adopted.

During a crisis, decisions need to be made urgently and there may be no time to consult others. In such cases a telling or selling style is likely to be appropriate. On the other hand a task that is easily structured and defined may lend itself to participating and delegating styles.

◆ **The motivation and ability of staff**

❖ What is a person's level of motivation and confidence?

❖ Does the person have the skills or competence needed?

Low levels of motivation and ability suggest a telling style, whereas high levels of motivation and ability suggest a delegating style.

During change you can choose an appropriate leadership style to develop the motivation and commitment and skills of your team members and increase their involvement in the change.

When a member has	Appropriate style	Effect
Low levels of motivation and skills	**Telling** – controlling the task	Ensure success for the task and for the team member, helping to build both skills and motivation
Low skills, but is willing and motivated	**Selling** – retaining control while explaining and discussing what needs to be done and why	Control to ensure success, while building on the enthusiasm to develop skills
High skills, but unmotivated	**Participating** – giving a lot of support and encouragement	Demonstrate confidence in the team member to build motivation
High skills and high motivation	**Delegating** – giving ownership to the team member, being available to offer support where needed	Trust the team member to take control and succeed

Activity

Put yourself in these short scenarios:

Restructuring in your organisation has led to redundancies and the formation of new teams. It has happened very quickly, and although the members of your new team are relieved still to be part of the organisation, they are uncertain and anxious about their new role.

What leadership style would you use with them at this stage?

You have recently been appointed team leader of a customer service team. Your investigations show that there is a high level of customer complaints. You think that the way that the team processes customer orders may have something to do with the large number of complaints and you want to change it. You are about to have a team meeting.

What leadership style do you take at the team meeting?

As the team leader of the new team in the first scenario you may feel that the team needs some reassurance and direction at first, with a clear focus on what the team exists to do. A telling style may be appropriate, while promoting good communications by encouraging feedback and questions. If team members ask questions about the team's purpose you can move to a selling style – explaining your decisions and providing an opportunity for clarification and further exploration of the change.

In the second scenario you may use a participating style to encourage team members to contribute their ideas about the problems customers face. As long as they don't feel defensive, or worried that they will be blamed they will probably welcome the recognition that they have a valuable perspective on customer service issues.

The theories

An interest in what makes leaders and managers effective led to some important studies of managers and leaders in the 1960s and 1970s and a swathe of leadership models and theories dealing with leadership style. Some of these include:

◆ Tannenbaum and Schmidt's continuum of management behaviour

◆ Vroom and Yetton's contingency model

◆ Blake and Mouton's leadership grid

◆ Hersey and Blanchard's situational leadership model.

For more information on these theories, see the References section at the end of this book.

The discussion of leadership style in this chapter draws on the work of these researchers and theorists.

Support your staff

To show support to your people you need to communicate and listen – openly, honestly and often. Here are some ideas:

◆ Show your own commitment to the change throughout the process.

◆ Treat people fairly.

◆ Show an interest in people and the work they contribute.

◆ Take action early to deal with problems.

◆ Encourage people by showing trust and giving them responsibility.

◆ Provide people with development opportunities.

◆ Explore and discuss plans, where appropriate.

◆ Ensure people have the resources needed, including information, time, equipment, access to other people and parts of the organisation.

◆ Make yourself available and be approachable.

◆ Ask how things are going and review progress both in formal meetings and informal discussions.

◆ Give positive and constructive feedback where appropriate.

◆ Use praise and thanks to recognise and acknowledge effort and performance.

◆ Be prepared to give advice, make suggestions and be decisive to move forward.

◆ Recognise and celebrate success.

The best way to inspire people to superior performance is to convince them by everything you do and by your everyday attitude that you are wholeheartedly supporting them.

Harold S. Geneen

The level and quality of support offered to team members will depend on your leadership style and the particular needs of team members. For example, if you are delegating, your team member will expect to be trusted to get on with the task. If you then suggest a meeting to take a look at the team member's plans, you risk undermining that presumed level of trust. On the other hand if you are working with someone who lacks confidence, high levels of support are likely to be welcomed.

Summary

◆ The carrot and stick approaches are two extremes of attitudes of leaders and managers. Their attitudes will affect the response of team members and their ability to lead change.

◆ As a leader you need to keep an open mind and develop your understanding and self-awareness. Reflect on events to challenge your assumptions.

◆ Team members will be watching you and take you as a role model.

◆ Good communication is open, two-way and about building understanding.

◆ Six planning questions help you to achieve your aims in communicating. The most important one is 'What do the people receiving your message need?'

◆ Listen carefully to encourage your team members to express their feelings and to show your understanding and acceptance.

◆ Use open questions to encourage people to speak.

◆ You can involve people right at the start of change, and in shaping it. When this is not possible, involve them in shaping the consequences of change.

◆ Involving team members encourages them to invest in the change and to take some control. It gives them a real stake in the change: they want to make it work.

◆ To encourage team members to become involved:

  ❖ Get to know the concerns of your team members

  ❖ Focus attention and effort on the task

  ❖ Adapt your leadership style

  ❖ Support your staff.

5 Implementing change

Introduction

You use leadership skills to help people accept that change is going to happen, overcome their resistance and become involved in the change. One of the most useful ways of involving people is by focusing their attention on the task. You will want to encourage team members to contribute to planning what needs to be done to achieve the desired future situation and enable them to implement the change.

A process of planning and implementing allows for some control over change. The process involves:

◆ Setting and agreeing objectives that are linked to the vision and goals for change.

◆ Planning the detail of what needs to be done, and the required resources.

◆ Implementing the plans while monitoring progress carefully.

◆ With the information from monitoring, you can make changes to the plan or modify your actions in order to ensure that you still achieve your objectives or continue on the road towards them.

Controlling the implementation of change

◆ Reviewing progress to identify what has been achieved, what has been learned and what, if anything, still needs to be done to achieve the vision.

This chapter focuses on each stage of the process. You will find out:

◆ About creating a link between the vision and the objectives you set.

◆ How to set and agree SMART objectives that include appropriate measures.

◆ About breaking work down into tasks and identifying resource requirements.

◆ How to support implementation and monitoring.

◆ About reviewing what has been learned.

But we start by looking at the nature of planning change.

Ah, I see great change ahead, you must start planning NOW...

The nature of planning change

Manage the risks

Making changes means moving to unknown territory. Uncertainty means that change involves risk. You can reduce the risks by planning. But it is important first to understand the risks you face and seek to manage them in the way you plan change.

Risk can arise from:

◆ **The outcome not meeting expectations**

There is always a risk that the work to implement change will not deliver the results intended.

◆ **People**

Will people succeed in the tasks they have to carry out? Do they have the skills, understanding and commitment to implement the change? Do managers have the ability to galvanise action and support it?

◆ **Timing**

Is the timing of the change under your control or governed by external considerations – delivery times, events in other parts of the organisation, for example? How confident are you in your ability to estimate the time needed to implement change? Inaccurate estimates can cause missed deadlines, and can adversely affect people and the availability of other resources.

◆ **Other resources**

New technology, overstretched equipment and facilities, insufficient funds can all lead to delays, halt progress and undermine achievements.

It is worth considering the risks you face and how damaging they can be if they occur. Here is a simple approach, which is based on your subjective judgement of the change.

Tackle the risks

The next stage is to work out how to tackle these risks to minimise the likelihood of them occurring and their consequences if they do.

There may be several options:

◆ **Avoid the risk**. For example you may be able to pass the risk onto someone else by contracting part of the work to an external expert who is better skilled and experienced to handle the risk. You may be able to reorganise the implementation of change to avoid some of your risks.

◆ **Reduce the risk**. You can ensure your preparation and planning are geared to making it less likely that a risk will occur.

◆ **Accept the risk**. This means contingency planning – allowing extra finance to allocate additional resources if necessary and some slack in the schedule.

Activity

For a change you are facing, first assess the risks and then consider what you can do to manage them.

Managing the risks you face comes down to planning.

Planning

Planning gives some control over the process and outcomes of a change. It involves thinking through and recording what you want to achieve and how you are going to do it. Plans themselves provide a means for communicating and monitoring the tasks that need to be done and the resources required.

The people who draw up plans will depend on their:

◆ Experience, knowledge and judgement together with the advice of others who have been involved in similar situations.

◆ Assessment of the resources they have at their disposal.

◆ Understanding of likely events that could have an impact on what they want to achieve.

◆ Ability to allocate appropriate resources, including other people, to achieve the desired outcome.

In spite of the expertise at the heart of planning, it is always based on anticipation and supposition, in other words educated guesswork.

In reality it isn't at all surprising when 'things don't go according to plan', especially during change. Of course this doesn't make planning a worthless activity. What it does do is highlight the need for plans to be flexible and easily adapted. This means that the people who are working to make change happen need to be able to:

◆ Recognise when there are problems – when the planned actions aren't contributing to the required outcomes or when events occur that affect the plans.

◆ Keep an open mind to question the validity of a plan.

◆ Act decisively when required.

◆ Deal positively with setbacks.

◆ Modify plans and actions in the light of new information.

◆ Keep communicating – both formally and informally – so that people know what is happening and why.

Plans can provide the best guide, but they must be reshaped and modified while they are being used.

To ensure that plans provide the best guide, however, it is important to make sure they are closely linked to what you want to achieve.

From goals to objectives to plans

The vision and goals for change give direction and purpose. They provide the basis for planning and action. Everyone affected by a change has to find out how they can and ought to contribute to achieving the vision and goals. They stimulate these questions:

What do the vision and goals mean for our department, team and for me?

What do we have to achieve?

What behaviours and actions are needed?

In answering these questions, people interpret and expand the overall goals and develop concrete and specific objectives for achieving the change. In turn the objectives provide a basis for developing detailed plans. The plans and objectives all head in the same direction and all make some contribution to achieving the overall vision and goals. This alignment of goals is sometimes known as a hierarchy of objectives.

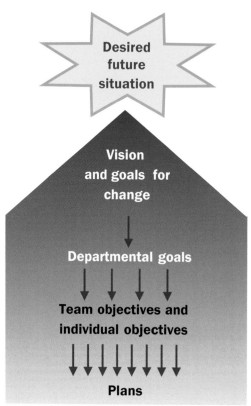

A hierarchy of objectives

As the goals are translated and expanded onto objectives they become more detailed and specify the standards and behaviour required to achieve them.

A word about terminology

Bear in mind that different words may be used to describe goals and objectives. For example, aim or purpose may be used instead of goal, and goals or targets may be used instead of objectives.

Whatever terminology you use, the main thing to recognise is that the broad statements of what you want to achieve are expanded to be described in progressively greater detail.

In this book we use goals for the broad statements, objectives for more detailed descriptions of what needs to be done. Plans show how the work is to be done.

I would like you all to review your purpose during the third and forth quartile to ensure an upturn in achieving our objectives.

Setting and agreeing objectives

> Objectives focus on *what* needs to be done and to what standard.

An objective is derived from a broader goal, and states in detail what has to be done in order to contribute to the goal. It also gives the standard to be met, so that it is possible to check progress and see how far it has been achieved.

You can use quantifiable and qualitative measures to show the standards that have to be applied.

Measures and standards

Quantifiable measures

These are based on hard data – the number, amount or degree of something:

◆ Make 10 new sales contacts in a week.

◆ Run training sessions for 16 people on how to use the new knowledge management system for £150 per person per day.

◆ Increase fertiliser production by 150 tonnes per week.

◆ Improve punctuality of deliveries by 10 per cent.

These measures are relatively easy to set when you can draw on available data, such as: the average number of sales contacts made by the top 20 performing sales staff in a week during the past quarter; the general cost of training; supply capacity, customer demand for fertiliser; and historic data about punctuality from within the company.

Quantifiable measures are also straightforward to test – you compare actual results with those specified. This allows you to monitor performance quickly.

Qualitative measures

These are based on the character or quality of something. They often relate to people's behaviour or attitudes. As such they depend on people's subjective assessment and opinion of what matters:

- Run a training session that gives trainees the understanding and confidence they need to start using the new knowledge management system.

- Agree a new team communication process so that every team member is kept informed of progress.

- Establish a new code of conduct for the sales team that meets customer and organisational requirements.

To establish and test qualitative measures, you have to use judgement, based on people's considered opinions and views, observation and experience. Qualitative measures may include required behaviours and skills. As an example, consider the measures for running a training session.

A training session

Run a training session that gives trainees the understanding and confidence they need to start using the new knowledge management system.

To establish these measures, you may need to discuss with the trainers the scope and limits of the training, and identify in detail what people generally need in terms of understanding and confidence in order to start using the new system.

You can test whether the objective has been achieved in several ways. To test whether they have the confidence they need, you may use observation to see how far trainees start using the new system, record the type of queries that arise and have post-training discussions with trainees to find out their level of comfort in using the system and with the training.

Sometimes you can convert qualitative into quantitative data and use this as the basis to test an objective. However, this can be costly and time-consuming to gather. Look at the training session example again:

You could use a multiple-choice quiz to check that trainees have the required knowledge and understanding to use the system. You could also ask trainees to complete a questionnaire to rate their confidence in using the system. The trainees' scores and ratings deliver quantitative data which help in assessing whether the objective has been achieved.

When deciding which measures and standards to use to support an objective, it is worth considering its costs and benefits. Think about:

◆ How easy the measure is to apply

◆ How relevant it is to the work being done

◆ What resources – time, money, etc. – will be needed to use it

◆ How useful it will be to apply that measure – immediately and in the long term.

Consider the training sessions example again:

Is it worth using quizzes and questionnaires to check the effectiveness of the sessions? It is time-consuming, but it may provide data that could be used to support further training in future. On the other hand, such training may not have a long-term role. In such a case it may be simpler and more effective to make a judgement based on how far trainees start using the new system.

Using measures during change

Many people apply standards and measures rigidly. However, during change, quantifiable measures may not be easy to set reliably, especially if the data is scarce or irrelevant to the new situation. You may have to draw on estimates or assumptions about what will work, and you may find qualitative measures more suitable. It is important to be clear about expected standards of performance, such as how people need to behave to customers and colleagues, but during change it may be wise to use measures as a *guide* rather than as a *test* of success.

Activity

Note some examples of quantifiable measures and qualitative measures you have used to check progress in a change you have experienced.

◆ How relevant do you think they are?

◆ Are they worth testing, given the costs of doing so?

◆ Are there simpler measures you can use?

You may find it useful to discuss your ideas with colleagues.

SMART objectives

One way of setting objectives is to write them so that they meet a number of criteria:

Specific - They state clearly what has to be achieved

Measurable - They include measures or standards by which you can monitor and assess progress.

Achievable - They are feasible and realistic to achieve, given the resources available - skills, equipment, time, information, etc.

Relevant - They must contribute to the broad purpose or aims of the team or department and be seen as relevant by the people tasked with undertaking them

Time-bound - They are tied to a deadline.

These are known as SMART, after the first letter of each of these criteria. Here is an example:

Goal: 'to improve customer service'

One objective that contributes to this goal is: 'to identify and communicate customer service problems to the team.' This could be made into the following SMART objective:

To identify and communicate customer service problems to the team for agreement and action:

Analyse customer service problems experienced by the team over the past 18 months drawing on customer service and complaints records and discussions with customer service staff. Report the findings, highlighting up to three main problem areas. At the team meeting on 12 April deliver a short (up to 10 minutes) presentation of the main problem areas, supported by a written report, and lead a team discussion to agree what action to take next.

In this example you can see that the objective is specific, measurable, relevant and time-bound. It appears to be achievable given the customer service records and access to customer service staff.

However, whether or not it is achievable in practice will depend on the skills of the person who is charged with achieving it, and whether or not that person supports and agrees with the objective.

Choose a goal for change that you need to achieve. Write an objective that will contribute to achieving the goals and restate it as a SMART objective.

Involving people in setting objectives

> You have to ensure individuals agree to objectives if you expect them to put in energy and effort to achieving them.

In writing SMART objectives you are thinking through precisely what needs to be achieved. Change can mean moving into unfamiliar territory and you may benefit from involving others. By involving people in setting and writing explicit objectives you:

◆ Pool knowledge, expertise and experience which helps to ensure the objective is appropriate and SMART.

◆ Gain people's support and agreement for the objectives, which makes it easier for them to be committed to achieving them.

To involve people, use a leadership style that is matched to the individuals' levels of motivation and competence. Your aim is to increase confidence and gain agreement with the objective so that the person is encouraged to succeed.

We looked at leadership style in Chapter 4 on Leadership, page 84.

Using an appropriate leadership style to agree objectives

When you are working with an experienced team member who is anxious about change, you could take a participative style:

◆ Discuss the scope and limits of the task with the individual

◆ Ask him or her to draft their own SMART objectives

◆ Meet with the team member to review jointly and finally agree the objectives.

When you are working with those who lack experience, you could use a selling style, explaining and discussing the SMART objectives with them, exploring the measures, discussing how they might tackle the job, and ensuring that they have the resources and ongoing support needed to achieve the objectives.

Planning the detail

When you have agreed SMART objectives you can develop detailed plans. These show the tasks that need to be done to achieve the objectives.

> Plans show *how* the work is to be done

Planning the work that needs to be done involves:

◆ Breaking down complex tasks into smaller ones so that they become manageable

◆ Putting them into an appropriate order

◆ Estimating resource requirements for each task

◆ Communicating and agreeing the plans.

Breal work down to manageable small tasks

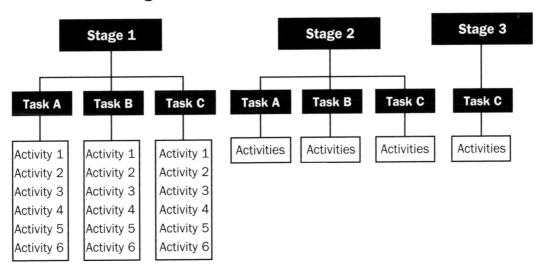

Break down the work

The main stages are first identified. These are then divided into tasks. Then each task is broken down into smaller activities.

Tips for breaking down the work

1 Think about how you can involve other people. You could run a brainstorming session with your team or you could ask a group of team members to break down the work for a particular stage of the plan and then jointly review the results.

2 List all the stages required to achieve your objectives.

3 Then list all the tasks that need to be done to complete a stage.

4 Taking each task in turn, list all the activities that are needed to complete a task. Do not forget that a task may need approval before it can be signed off and completed, so an activity may be to approve something.

5 Check that you have identified all the appropriate tasks by asking:

◆ When all the activities for a particular task are completed will the task itself be completed?

◆ When all these stages and tasks completed will we have achieved our objectives?

◆ Are all the tasks clearly stated so everyone knows what the task involves?

◆ Are all the tasks necessary?

Put the tasks in order

When you have a list of all the stages, tasks and activities, you can put them in order by thinking about the logical sequence for completing a series of activities. Identify:

◆ **Initial tasks**. These are the tasks and activities that need to be done first.

◆ **Dependent tasks**. Some activities or tasks have to be completed before another can start:

Task A → Activity 1 → Activity 2 → Activity 3 → Activity 4

Initial tasks   Dependent tasks

♦ **Simultaneous tasks**. Some activities are independent from others and can take place at the same time as others.

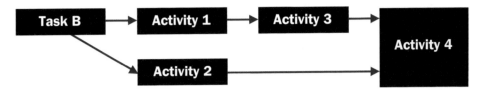

Estimate resource requirements

The next part of planning is to estimate the resources required to complete each activity and task. These may include:

♦ **People and skills** – the number of people needed do the task, the skills required to do it, and who has those skills.

♦ **Finance** – you may need to cost your tasks, for example, the cost of external expertise, renting a room for a meeting.

♦ **Equipment and materials** – including access to meeting rooms, computer equipment, vehicles, supplies, information.

♦ **Time** – the hours or days it will take to complete the task given the resources available; this is different from the total number of days from the start to the end of the job.

Estimates may be based on prior experience and assumptions of what may be involved, discussions with other people such as suppliers.

The people who are to carry out a particular task may be best placed to estimate the resources required, because of their particular expertise and experience. But even if their background gives little direct help in identifying resources for the task ahead they need to own it and feel that it is feasible, so should be involved in estimating resource requirements.

Consider your priorities. If you want results quickly you may need to put additional resources into tasks. This may be a useful approach right at the start of the implementation process in order to create some momentum and to deliver some early successes.

Also consider how much scope you have to plan for contingencies. For example, is it desirable or possible to have some slack in the deadline for completing stages? Can you access extra resources if you need to?

Communicate and agree the plans

Plans are the working documents for action. But they are also the basis for agreement and support.

You must make sure your team members understand their role and responsibilities, what they are expected to achieve and how they are expected to behave. You have to get their agreement and that of other stakeholders, such as your managers, suppliers and customers, before you can proceed.

Plans ought to be clear and easy to read so that people can understand them quickly and put them to use.

Planning charts

Project management software can be useful in planning and setting out plans. One of the key advantages of using an automated method for planning is that such plans are easily modified. When you make a change to one part of the plan, for example, the rest of the plan is automatically updated and you can see the knock-on effects of making the change. This gives you scope for trying out different ways of allocating resources to find the best approach.

You can also use simple charts for presenting plans, developed using spreadsheets or word-processing packages. These are not so easily updated but they can sometimes be easier to read. Two examples are a chart showing resource requirements and a Gantt chart.

The following extract is from a chart that shows the resource estimates for each activity:

Resource requirements

Activity	Person responsible	Other people involved	Time required	Equipment	Materials	Cost
2.1 Agree functions & contents	JG	TW NA PN JAD PD AC LK	½ day	Meeting room	OHP Computer Flip chart Report on website requirements	n/a

A chart like this gives a clear record which is easily shared and communicated to others.

A Gantt chart lists the tasks and activities and shows when each should start and how long it will take to complete. Here is an extract from a Gantt chart showing some of the activities for designing a new website:

2 Design new website	July				August
	1-6	8-13	15-19	22-27	30-4
2.1 Agree functions & contents	▪				
2.2 Finalise designer brief	▬				
2.3 Select designer	▬				
2.4 Commission/brief designer		▬			
2.5 Develop sample mockups			▬		
2.6 Deliver sample				▬	
2.7 Agree/approve sample					▬

In this chart you can quickly see the anticipated sequence and flow of activities. Notice, for example, the activity to select a designer can take place while the designer brief is being finalised.

Gantt charts show at a glance what is expected to happen and when. They show when there are gaps in activity and when there may be overload.

You can use Gantt charts to track and record what actually happens and compare this to the plan, which you can update accordingly.

When you present the plans, bear in mind what they are for. Have a look at this story – rather a cautionary tale.

A cautionary tale

'My manager was meticulous. He invested in some sophisticated project management software and produced glorious and numerous plans for the change project we were about to start: detailed Gantt charts, network diagrams, critical path analyses, charts of roles and responsibilities... They took him ages to sort out.

'We never really used them, though. They were too complicated to follow and actually didn't have much bearing on reality, which was much less clear cut and more about agreeing something, getting on and doing it and keeping everyone involved in the picture.'

Choose planning charts that are:

◆ Easy to prepare

◆ Easy to understand

◆ Easy to use for tracking

◆ Easy to update/modify.

Using planning charts

◆ Make sure that they don't become so complex that they are difficult to read.

◆ Check that the people who need to refer to the plans can access and read them.

◆ Decide who is authorised to update the plans.

◆ Control the versions of the plan and have a clear process for communicating updated versions.

Think about methods for presenting plans that you have used in the past and any other methods available to you.

Decide which of these methods is most suitable for your purposes.

When you draw up your plans bear in mind that the documents themselves are merely tools. What really matters is actually getting down to the work - implementing the change.

Implementing change

During implementation your role will include:

◆ Keeping team members and other stakeholders up-to-date

◆ Coordinating effort and ensuring resources are available

◆ Listening to and supporting the people carrying out the tasks

◆ Keeping a focus on the overall picture – what you are working to achieve

◆ Creating a positive atmosphere

◆ Maintaining energy and motivation.

In addition your focus will be on monitoring and dealing with problems. You may also have to deal with conflict.

Monitoring

The purpose of monitoring is to:

◆ Check progress against SMART objectives.

◆ Record actual progress against planned progress.

◆ Identify problems or potential problems early.

Monitoring may reveal any number of problems, such as:

◆ The activities and tasks are not achieving the objectives.

◆ The change has unexpected negative outcomes.

◆ The work is falling behind schedule.

◆ Resource estimates are inaccurate.

◆ A change in personnel or other unforeseen events disrupt the implementation.

Monitoring enables you to take prompt action to deal with such problems to keep the work on track to achieve the vision and goals.

Ways of tackling these problems could include:

◆ Changing the plans to reflect new circumstances

- Revisiting objectives and rewriting them
- Amending resource allocation to activities
- Changing activities or introducing new ones.

Ways of monitoring

Encourage people to monitor their own work as far as possible. You can check progress formally through:

- **Reports and records**, such as Gantt charts that track progress against the plan.

- **Regular team meetings**. These keep everyone informed of progress and can allow people to share experiences, and to explore difficulties.

- **One-to-one progress report meetings**. These are useful for individuals who lack experience or confidence. They allow you to focus on one part of the project in detail and to provide specific support and guidance to individuals.

You can also keep an eye on what is happening informally by:

- Listening and talking to people. This used to be known as *managing by walking about*. It implies taking time to go and talk to people and observing them at work. It can still be an effective approach, but today you may need to pick up a phone to keep in touch with people.

- Keeping your door open and being available.

Case study

I worked on a change project, designing a development project for a large organisation. I worked from home, but I was still part of the team and was in close contact with other people by phone and email. My manager let me get on with my work. She never contacted me unless she wanted something. We didn't have much social chitchat. On the other hand, I could always contact her if I wanted to discuss something. If I couldn't reach her on her mobile, she always returned the call.

Your approach to monitoring will depend on the level of control and trust you give to other people.

Think about a change you recently experienced at work:

◆ What monitoring data was generated during implementation?

◆ How far was self-monitoring encouraged?

◆ How did the team leader or manager keep informed about progress and potential problems?

◆ Do you think the level of monitoring was appropriate?

◆ What, if anything, would you do differently with your team now?

Dealing with problems

Monitoring may highlight a range of problems or issues that result from moving into unknown territory. Your team members are likely to be the among the first to encounter any difficulties that highlight unintended and negative consequences of change.

It is important to take decisive action in the face of problems both to:

◆ Maintain progress in achieving the overall goals and vision

◆ Show support to your team.

Explore complaints

◆ Show that you respect the views and opinions of team members.

◆ Listen to stories or explanations from team members that suggest dissatisfaction with aspects of the change.

◆ Take the views of your team seriously. Don't ignore or dismiss reported difficulties.

◆ Be prepared to investigate further by collecting more information about the issue and assessing the consequences – impact on staff and customers, impact on work processes, costs and so on.

◆ Consider whether you can deal with the issue in your work area or whether it is to do with organisational processes and systems and needs to be reported to management.

By showing your team you are interested in their concerns and take their views seriously you will build trust between you. However, consider how to balance the desire to give a strong direction and take decisive action with the importance of involving other people. Whenever possible, avoid taking ownership of a task away from another person.

You may be able to engage in joint problem-solving for many of the problems arising from monitoring. Use the following approach.

An approach to problem-solving

Ask the following questions:

◆ What is the nature of the problem? Gather the facts.

◆ Whose problem is it to solve?

◆ What are the possible causes of the problem?

◆ Who can you usefully consult?

◆ What information do you need? What information is available?

◆ What are your best options to solve the problem? For each consider:

  ❖ Will it work?

  ❖ Is it acceptable to the people involved?

◆ Which is the best option? This is your solution.

◆ Reflect on your approach and make the decision.

Dealing with conflict

Conflict can be creative and constructive when it concerns the task and when people respect each other. Disagreements can lead to better decisions. However, when people work closely together to achieve an objective, and particularly when they feel under pressure, their style, approach and priorities may clash, causing destructive conflict. Such a conflict may lead to arguments and emotional outbursts that are personally insulting. A difficult atmosphere may result, with an inability to work together.

Although you can't force people to overcome their differences, your concern for getting the job done and for the overall atmosphere in the team means that you can't ignore the conflict.

There are five approaches to dealing with conflict:

1 **Avoidance** – avoiding each other.

2 **Accommodation** – apologising and standing down from one's own position

3 **Confrontation** – demanding apologies and some kind of recompense

4 **Compromise** – finding a way for both parties to save face.

5 **Collaboration** – focusing on joint problem-solving

The first three approaches may be short-term solutions, but they don't help to solve the conflict in the long term; indeed they may build resentment between the parties. Compromise may be acceptable, but a more satisfactory approach, especially where people have to work together, is to collaborate in joint problem-solving.

Ideas for resolving conflict

- Allow people some time and distance from each other to get over the immediate hurt and lost tempers.

- Encourage both parties to agree to meet with the aim of resolving their differences and finding a way forward.

- Take the role of a mediator.

- Focus on the facts and be impartial.

- Encourage each person to take turns to express their opinions openly.

- Encourage each person to listen to the other's view.

- Help people to see the situation from the other person's point of view.

- Give people a structured problem-solving approach to finding a way through their conflict.

Think about the ideas given here for dealing with conflict and your own experiences of conflict at work, either first-hand or as a team leader or manager.

How far you could use these ideas for helping people overcome conflict during change?

What other ideas could you use?

You may agree that a team leader's ability to deal successfully with conflict among team members will depend on the level of credibility he or she has among team members. Key to this is the team leader's respect and concern for people.

Reviewing and learning

Change means learning new skills, new behaviours, new ways of doing things. Reviewing enables you to capture what you have learned.

Reviewing is an opportunity to step back from change and assess what has happened.

Reviewing is part of the process to control and implement change.

Controlling the implementation of change

It is an important activity in all types of change, allowing you to assess the impact and the process of change, and look ahead at what needs to happen next.

Reviewing may involve information gathering such as plans, monitoring data and the views and opinions of stakeholders.

You may be required to prepare a formal report reviewing the change. Alternatively you can use formal meetings as a way of conducting a review.

Questions for review

What have we achieved?

- Has the change achieved its goals and vision?
- What are the results of the change?
- What are the benefits of the change to the stakeholders?
- Is there anything still to achieve?
- What are we doing differently now?

How effective was the change process?

- What went well in planning and implementing change?
- What problems and obstacles were there?
- What would we do differently next time?

What have we learned?

- What have we learned in order to get where we are now?
- What have we learned about the process of change?

What next?

- What do we need to do next to achieve the vision and goals?
- What can we improve in the current situation?

Summary

◆ Change involves risk, so it is worth carrying out a simple risk assessment and working out how to manage the risks you face.

◆ Planning is a key approach for controlling and minimising risk, but plans are working documents – they must be reshaped and modified while they are being used.

◆ The vision and goals provide the basis for planning and action. They are expanded and translated into detailed objectives.

◆ Objectives should be SMART – specific, measurable, achievable, relevant and time-bound. They must also be agreed.

◆ Plans show how the objectives are to be achieved. Planning the detail involves: breaking down the work, putting tasks in order, estimating resources, communicating and agreeing the plans.

◆ Monitoring not only helps everyone keep track of progress but also allows the early detection of problems so that prompt action can be taken to maintain progress towards the vision and goals.

◆ Leaders need to be prepared to deal with problems, including complaints about negative effects of the change, and conflict situations.

◆ Reviewing gives the people involved in change the opportunity to assess its outcomes and process, and to capture what was learned.

References

Carnell, C. *Managing Change in Organizations*, 3rd edn. Prentice Hall Europe, 1999

Hersey, P. *The Situational Leader*, Leadership Studies Inc., 1984

Hersey, P. and Blanchard, K. H. *Management of Organizational Behaviour: Utilizing Human Resources*, 6th Edn, Prentice Hall, 1993

Kold, D. A. *Experiential Learning*, Prentice Hall, 1985

Lewin, K. *Field Theory in Social Science*, Harper and Row, 1952

McGregor, D. *The Human Side of Enterprise*, 3rd edn. Penguin, 1987

Mullins, L. J. *Management and Organizational Behaviour*, Financial TImes, Prentice Hall, 2005

Senge, P. et al. *The Fifth Discipline Fieldbook*, New York, Doubleday, 1994

Tannedbam, R. and Schmidt, W.H. 'How to choose a leadership pattern', *Harvard Business Review*, May-June 1973

Vroom, V. H. and Yetton, P. W. *Leadership and Decision Making*, University of Pittsburg Press, 1973.

Index

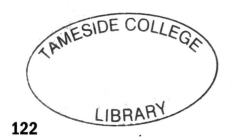